First World War
and Army of Occupation
War Diary
France, Belgium and Germany

2 CAVALRY DIVISION
Divisional Troops
3 Brigade Royal Horse Artillery
4 August 1914 - 29 September 1914,
15 March 1915 - 1 June 1915,
12 October 1915 - 29 December 1915
and 1 July 1916 - 1 February 1919

WO95/1123/1-4

The Naval & Military Press Ltd
www.nmarchive.com
Published in association with The National Archives

Published by

The Naval & Military Press Ltd

Unit 10 Ridgewood Industrial Park,

Uckfield, East Sussex,

TN22 5QE England

Tel: +44 (0) 1825 749494

www.naval-military-press.com

www.nmarchive.com

This diary has been reprinted in facsimile from the original. Any imperfections are inevitably reproduced and the quality may fall short of modern type and cartographic standards.

Contents

Document type	Place/Title	Date From	Date To
Heading	WO95/1123/1		
Heading	BEF 2 Cav Div Troops 3 Bde R.H.A		
Miscellaneous	H.Q., 3rd Bde. R.H.A.	08/02/1916	08/02/1916
Heading	1st Cavalry Divisional Artillery. Absorbed By H.Q.R.A. 2nd Cavalry Division 17.9.14. 3rd Brigade R.H.A. 4th August To 18th September 1914		
War Diary	Newbridge	04/08/1914	28/08/1914
War Diary	Pierremande	29/08/1914	29/08/1914
War Diary	Fontenoy	30/08/1914	30/08/1914
War Diary	Schelles	31/08/1914	31/08/1914
War Diary	Martfontaine	01/09/1914	01/09/1914
War Diary	Antilly	02/09/1914	02/09/1914
War Diary	Villenoy	03/09/1914	03/09/1914
War Diary	Chailly Ln Brie	05/09/1914	05/09/1914
War Diary	Vilbert	06/09/1914	06/09/1914
War Diary	Pezarches	07/09/1914	07/09/1914
War Diary	Les Potees	08/09/1914	08/09/1914
War Diary	J'hotel 1/2 S Of Le Grand Glairet	09/09/1914	09/09/1914
War Diary	Roogeville	10/09/1914	10/09/1914
War Diary	Passy	11/09/1914	11/09/1914
War Diary	Tigny	12/09/1914	12/09/1914
War Diary	Cheisseny	13/09/1914	14/09/1914
War Diary	Lime	15/09/1914	17/09/1914
War Diary	Braine	18/09/1914	23/09/1914
War Diary	WO95/1123/2		
Heading	BEF 2 Cav Div Troops 3 Bde R H A Ammo Col 1914 Aug To 1918 Feb		
Heading	1st Cavalry Divisional Artillery. Became 2nd Cavalry Divisional Ammunition Column 16.10.14 3rd Brigade R.H.A. Ammunition Column 5th August To 12th October 1914		
War Diary	Oldesnut	05/08/1914	03/10/1914
War Diary		29/09/1914	29/09/1914
War Diary	Commenced	15/03/1915	15/03/1915
War Diary	Vieux Berquin.	24/03/1915	13/04/1915
War Diary	Vieux Berquin		
War Diary	Vieux Berquin	15/03/1915	23/04/1915
War Diary	Boeschepe		
War Diary	Vlamertinghe	24/04/1915	24/04/1915
War Diary	1 Mile NW Of Brielen	25/04/1915	01/05/1915
War Diary	Reninghelst	02/05/1915	03/05/1915
War Diary	Le Sart	04/05/1915	04/05/1915
War Diary	Rue De Paradis Laventie		
War Diary	Laventie	10/05/1915	01/06/1915
War Diary	Norrent	12/10/1915	21/10/1915
War Diary	Thiembronne	24/10/1915	30/10/1915
War Diary	Lacouture	01/12/1915	10/12/1915
War Diary	Lacon	17/12/1915	19/12/1915
War Diary	Fosse	20/12/1915	29/12/1915

Heading	War Diary of 3rd Brigade R.H.A. from: 1st July to 31st July. 1916. (Volume		
War Diary	Hazebrouck	01/07/1916	26/07/1916
Heading	War Diary Of H.Q., 3rd Brigade R.H.A. For August 1916 Vol 2		
War Diary	Hazebrouck	01/08/1916	31/08/1916
Heading	War Diary Of Headquarters, 3rd Brigade R.H.A. For September, 1916, Vol III		
War Diary	Hazebrouck	01/09/1916	04/09/1916
War Diary	Busnes	06/09/1916	06/09/1916
War Diary	Sautrecourt	07/09/1916	07/09/1916
War Diary	Vieil Hesdin	08/09/1916	08/09/1916
War Diary	Remaisnil	10/09/1916	10/09/1916
War Diary	Vignacourt	11/09/1916	11/09/1916
War Diary	Bonnay	12/09/1916	14/09/1916
War Diary	Morlancourt	15/09/1916	30/09/1916
Heading	War Diary Of H.Q., 3rd Brigade, R.H.A. October, 1916. Vol 4		
War Diary	Meaulte	01/10/1916	10/10/1916
War Diary	400 S.E. High Wood	10/10/1916	27/10/1916
War Diary	Meaulte	28/10/1916	29/10/1916
Heading	War Diary Of Headquarters, 3rd Brigade, Royal Horse Artillery. November, 1916. Vol 5		
War Diary	Meaulte	01/11/1916	07/11/1916
War Diary	Bussy-Les-Daours.	08/11/1916	08/11/1916
War Diary	Belloy-Sur-Somme	09/11/1916	09/11/1916
War Diary	Gd Lawers	10/11/1916	11/11/1916
War Diary	Ligescourt	11/11/1916	26/11/1916
Heading	War Diary Of Headquarters, 3rd Brigade Royal Horse Artillery. December, 1916 Vol. 6		
War Diary	Crecy-Grange	01/12/1916	29/12/1916
Heading	War Diary Of Headquarters, 3rd Brigade R.H.A. January, 1917 Vol. XXIX. Vol 7		
War Diary	Crecy-Grange	01/01/1917	31/01/1917
Heading	War Diary Of Headquarters, 3rd Brigade, R.H.A. February, 1917. Vol XXX. Vol 8		
War Diary	Crecy Granges	01/02/1917	28/02/1917
Heading	War Diary Of Headquarters, Third Brigade, Royal Horse Artillery. March, 1917. Vol. XXXI. Vol 9		
War Diary	Crecy Grange	01/03/1917	31/03/1917
Heading	War Diary Of Headquarters, 3rd Brigade, R.H.A. April, 1917. Vol. XXXII. Vol 10		
War Diary	Grecy-Grange	01/04/1917	06/04/1917
War Diary	Wavans	07/04/1917	07/04/1917
War Diary	Henu	08/04/1917	09/04/1917
War Diary	1000 X S.W Of Tillon Les Marlaines	09/04/1917	11/04/1917
War Diary	Tilloy Les Mafflaines 1000 X SW	11/04/1917	11/04/1917
War Diary	Henu	12/04/1917	30/04/1917
Heading	War Diary Of Headquarters, 3rd Brigade, R.H.A May, 1917- Vol. XXXIII Vol XI		
War Diary	Henu	01/05/1917	14/05/1917
War Diary	Marquaix	15/05/1917	19/05/1917
War Diary	St Emelie	20/05/1917	31/05/1917
Heading	War Diary Of Headquarters 3rd Brigade RHA. From 1st June To 30th June 1917 Volume XXXIV. Vol 12		
War Diary	St Emelie	01/06/1917	30/06/1917

Heading	War Diary Of Headquarters 3rd Brigade RHA from 1st to 31st July 1917 Volume No XXXV. Vol. 13		
War Diary	St. Emelie	01/07/1917	09/07/1917
War Diary	Marquaix	10/07/1917	12/07/1917
War Diary	Suzanne	13/07/1917	16/07/1917
War Diary	Lucheux	17/07/1917	28/07/1917
War Diary	Bethune	29/07/1917	31/07/1917
Heading	War Diary Of 3rd Bde. R H A From 1st August To 31st August 1917 Volume XXXVI. Vol 14		
War Diary	Bethune	01/08/1917	31/08/1917
Heading	O.F. 3rd Brigade RHA	18/08/1917	18/08/1917
Miscellaneous	G.O.C., 2nd Cavalry Division. Appendix II	19/08/1917	19/08/1917
Heading	War Diary Of Headquarters 3rd Brigade RHA. From 1st to 30th September 1917 (Volume XXXVII) Vol 15		
War Diary	Gouey-En-Ternois	01/09/1917	07/09/1917
War Diary	Loos	08/09/1917	30/09/1917
Heading	War Diary Of Headquarters 3rd Brigade R.H.A From 1st October To 31st October 1917. Volume XXXVIII. Vol 16		
War Diary	Near Loos	01/10/1917	04/10/1917
War Diary	Loos	04/10/1917	07/10/1917
War Diary	Bracquemont	08/10/1917	08/10/1917
War Diary	Boyaval	09/10/1917	18/10/1917
War Diary	Houvin Houvie Neul	19/10/1917	19/10/1917
War Diary	Havernas	20/10/1917	20/10/1917
War Diary	Hebecourt	21/10/1917	22/10/1917
Heading	War Diary Of Headquarters 3rd Brigade RHA From 1st To 30th November 1917 Volume XXXIX. Vol 17		
War Diary	Rumigny	01/11/1917	15/11/1917
War Diary	Vaux Wood	16/11/1917	19/11/1917
War Diary	Gouzeav Court	20/11/1917	24/11/1917
War Diary	Dessart Wood	25/11/1917	26/11/1917
War Diary	Flesaueres	26/11/1917	29/11/1917
War Diary	Nr Flesquieres	30/11/1917	30/11/1917
Heading	War Diary Of Headquarters 3rd Brigade R.H.A. From 1st To 31st December 1917. Volume XL. Vol 18		
War Diary	Vendelles.	24/12/1917	31/12/1917
War Diary	Near Flesquieres	01/12/1917	03/12/1917
War Diary	Near Flesquieres	01/12/1917	04/12/1917
War Diary	Between Ribecourt & Havrincourt	05/12/1917	09/12/1917
War Diary	Vendelles	10/12/1917	31/12/1917
Heading	War Diary Of 3rd Bde. R.H.A. From 1st Jan. 1918 To 31 Jan. 1918 Volume 41. Vol 19		
War Diary	Vendelles	01/01/1918	31/01/1918
Heading	War Diary Of Headquarters 3rd Bde RHA. 1st-28th February 1918. Vol 20		
War Diary	Caulaincourt	01/02/1918	21/02/1918
War Diary	Maissemy	22/02/1918	28/02/1918
Heading	War Diary Of 3rd Brigade R.H.A. March 1918 Vol 21		
War Diary		01/03/1918	31/03/1918
Map	Enemy Sector Organization III		
Heading	Special Sheet H.Q. 3rd Brigade R.H.A		
War Diary	Gentelles	01/04/1918	01/04/1918
War Diary	Near Amiens	02/04/1918	05/04/1918
War Diary	Ailly-Le-Haut-Clocher	06/04/1918	06/04/1918
War Diary	Hun-Le-Chateau	10/04/1918	10/04/1918

War Diary	Bomy	12/04/1918	12/04/1918
War Diary	Blaringhem	13/04/1918	29/04/1918
War Diary	Coyecque	29/04/1918	30/04/1918
Heading	War Diary Of H.Q. 3rd Brigade R.H.A. May 1918 Vol XLV Vol 23		
War Diary	Coyecques	01/05/1918	05/05/1918
War Diary	Nimon Travel	05/05/1918	11/05/1918
War Diary	Nr Montcarrel	14/05/1918	26/05/1918
War Diary	Nr Montcarrel	25/05/1918	25/05/1918
Heading	War Diary H.Q. 3rd Brigade R.H.A. From 1st To 30th June 1918 Vol XLVI. Vol 24		
War Diary		01/06/1918	30/06/1918
Heading	War Diary Of Headquarters 3rd Brigade R.H.A. Volume 47. July 1918 Vol 25		
War Diary	Moncarrel Area	01/07/1918	01/07/1918
War Diary	Boubers Sur Canche	02/07/1918	02/07/1918
War Diary	Canaples	03/07/1918	03/07/1918
War Diary	Varennes	06/07/1918	07/07/1918
War Diary	Raincheval	08/07/1918	23/07/1918
War Diary	Moncarel Area	24/07/1918	31/07/1918
Miscellaneous	To. O.C. "D" Battery R.H.A.	19/07/1918	19/07/1918
Miscellaneous	March Table For 20th July 1918		
Heading	War Diary Of Headquarters 3rd Brigade R.H.A. From August 1st To August 31st 1918 Volume No 38 Vol 26		
Heading	Nature Of Enclosures		
War Diary	Montcavrel Area	01/08/1918	08/08/1918
War Diary	Nr Caix	09/08/1918	25/08/1918
Operation(al) Order(s)	2nd Cavalry Division Order No. 55	04/08/1918	04/08/1918
Operation(al) Order(s)	March Table for 4th/5th August 1918 issued with 2nd Cavalry Division Order No. 55		
Operation(al) Order(s)	2nd Cavalry Division Order No. 56	05/08/1918	05/08/1918
Operation(al) Order(s)	March Table for 5/6th August-Issued With 2nd Cav. Div. Order No. 56		
Operation(al) Order(s)	2nd Cavalry Division Order No. 57	06/08/1918	06/08/1918
Operation(al) Order(s)	March Table for night 6th/7th August issued with 2nd Cavalry Division Order No. 57		
Miscellaneous	3rd Cavalry Brigade.	06/08/1918	06/08/1918
Miscellaneous	2nd Cav. Div. G/161/1.		
Miscellaneous	2nd Cav. Div. G/161/1	06/08/1918	06/08/1918
Operation(al) Order(s)	2nd Cavalry Division Order No. 58	07/08/1918	07/08/1918
Operation(al) Order(s)	March Table for night 7th/8th August. Issued with 2nd Cavalry Division Order No. 58		
Miscellaneous	Very Secret.		
Heading	War Diary Of Headquarters, 3rd Bde, R.H.A. Volume 49 Vol 27		
War Diary	Gaudiempre	01/09/1918	06/09/1918
War Diary	Famechon	08/09/1918	16/09/1918
War Diary	Gaudiempre	17/09/1918	30/09/1918
Heading	War Diary Of Headquarters, 3rd Brigade. R.H.A. For October 1918. Volume 50 Vol 28		
War Diary	Gaudiempre	01/10/1918	31/10/1918
Heading	War Diary Of H.Q. 3rd Brigade R.H.A. November, 1918-Volume L.I Vol 29		
War Diary	Gaudiempre	01/11/1918	14/11/1918
War Diary	Taisnieres	15/11/1918	15/11/1918
War Diary	Douzies	17/11/1918	17/11/1918

War Diary	Thuin	18/11/1918	18/11/1918
War Diary	Morialme	21/11/1918	21/11/1918
War Diary	Dinant	22/11/1918	22/11/1918
War Diary	Barcinalle	23/11/1918	23/11/1918
War Diary	Waha	24/11/1918	30/11/1918
Heading	War Diary Of Headquarters, 3rd Brigade R.H.A. From 1st December, 1918 To 31st December, 1918 Volume LII Vol 30		
War Diary	Waha	01/12/1918	28/12/1918
Heading	War Diary Of Headquarters, 3rd Brigade R.H.A. 2nd Cavalry Division From 1st To 31st January 1919. Volume 53. Vol 31		
War Diary	Hodbomont	01/01/1919	01/01/1919
Heading	War Diary Of Headquarters, 3rd Brigade R.H.A. From 1st To 28th February 1919. Volume 54. Vol 32		
War Diary	Hodbomont Theux Belgium	01/02/1919	01/02/1919

BEF

2 CAV DIV TROOPS

3 BDE R.H.A

1914 AUG & SEPT
1915 MAR to 1915 MAY
1915 OCT " 1915 DEC
1916 JULY " 1919 FEB

FOR "D" BATTERY See Box 1133
" J BATTERY See Box 1135
" E " " " 1139

Confid

CONFIDENTIAL

A.G.'s OFFICE AT THE [illegible]
CENTRAL REGI[S]TRY
-9 FEB 1916
C.R. No. 140/858

3 Bde R.H.A. 12th October to 31st December 1915.

H.Q.,

3rd Bde. R.H.A.

- - - - - - - - - - - - - -

With reference to the enclosed War Diary, will you please say what Volume it is to be numbered, no previous Diaries having apparently been received.

War Diaries from "D", "E" and "J" Batteries and the Ammunition Column of the Brigade have been received regularly.

G.H.Q.,
3rd Echelon.
8-2-16.

[signature] Major,
D.A.A.G.,
for D. A. G.,

D.A.A.G.

Owing to various active service conditions I am afraid I can't say what has been done with previous diaries. They may have been sent to Records at home & I am making enquiries. Meanwhile the only thing to do appears to be to start a new volume.

J. G. Oliviant[?]
Lt Col R.H.A.
Comm. 3rd Bde R.H.A.

I suppose you have not got them classified by any chance under the heading 2nd Cav. Division? [illegible]

1st Cavalry Divisional Artillery.

ABSORBED BY H. Q. R. A. 2nd CAVALRY DIVISION 17.9.14.

3rd BRIGADE R. H. A.

4th AUGUST to 18th SEPTEMBER 1914.

W A R D I A R Y
or
INTELLIGENCE SUMMARY (Vide F.S.Regns:

Hour, Date, Place.	Summary of Events and Information	Remarks and references to Appemdices
Aug. 4th 1914 Newbridge.	Mobilization ordered 5.30 p.m. — Pre. Day	3rd Brigade, RHA: Attached 3rd Cav. Bde.
Aug 5th 1914 —	Mob. continued — A. C. parked & wagons filled. 1st Day. JGB	The Officers for A.C came from Brigade at Woolwich — 112 men from Brigade Ipswich 143 horses from Brigade at Aldershot This seems an unnecessary complication. They might all have come from one Brigade & would have known something of each other — Both Offrs i/c Details & their Staff removed by I. C. orders — Any handing over rendered impossible —
Aug 6th 1914 — —	Mob continued — Subsidized horses bad — 112 men from 6th Bde Ipswich. JGB	
Aug 7 — —	Mob continued — Horses of Brigade completed — Reservists joined — JGB	
Aug 8th — —	Mob continued — Brigade complete — JGB	
Aug 9th — —	Ditto. Brigade separated into Units proceeding on Service — 1st Reinforcement Details left behind — JGB	
Aug 10th —	Brigade marched out complete Reported as mobilization complete JGB	

A R D I A R Y
or
LLIGENCE SUMMARY (Vide F.S. Regns:)

Hour, Date, Place.	Summary of Events and Information	Remarks and references to Appemdices
Aug 11th Newbridge.	No orders to move received —	Made up picketing ropes are no use for Artillery — They cannot JKG stand being tied to wagons.
Aug 12th Newbridge.	No orders to move.	
Aug 13th Newbridge.	" " " "	
Aug 14th " "	" " " Orders received to entrain on Saturday	
Aug 15th	Brigade entrained at Newbridge Curragh Siding, embarked at DUBLIN NORTH WALL	
Aug 16	Sailed during night 15/16th on SS. ATLANTIAN. ARCHIMEDES. PANCRAS	
Aug 17	At sea.	
Aug 18th	Arrived at HAVRE — night 17/18th.	
Aug 19th	Entrained for concentration area. 4 trains	
Aug 20th	Arrived at HAUTMONT & billeted at QUIEVELON	

Y

(...de F.S.Regns:)

Hour, Date, Place.	Summary of Events and Information	Remarks and references to Appemdices
Aug. 21st	Marched to HARMIGNIES via GIVRY. Prepared gun positions above HARMIGNIES but did not come into action	First portion ext'd and sent to M.
Aug. 22nd	Both batteries fired a few rounds near BRAY. E shelled by enemy. 2 horses hit. Night march to QUIEVRAIN. Billets.	
Aug 23rd	In billets, ready to turn out.	
Aug 24th	In action against Germans advancing. E Battery in the open heavily shelled vide St Palmer, but no casualties. Both batteries fired with success against Germans. Retired by sections with some difficulty.	
Aug 25th	Marched with column during the day & did a night march to LE CATEAU but marched out again & encamped in a field outside. Marched again at dawn.	
Aug 26th	Retired all day covering rear guard of infantry. Came into action near BUSIGNY & did a night march to D'ORVILLIERS	

W A R D I A R Y
or
INTELLIGENCE SUMMARY (Vide F.S.Regns:)

Hour, Date, Place.	Summary of Events and Information	Remarks and references to Appemdices
Aug. 27th	Night march thro' St QUENTIN. Horses & men very tired	
Aug 28th		
Aug 29th PIERREMONDE	Marched all day	
Aug 30th FONTENOY	marched all day to FONTENOY & spent the night there.	
Aug 31st SCHELLES	Moved away from FONTENOY & marched via AMBLENY	
Sept 1st ~~[illegible]~~. MORTFONTAINE	One Section D in action.	

R Y

SUMMARY (Vide F.S.Regn

Hour, Date, Place.	Summary of Events and Information	Remarks and references to Appemdices
Sept 2d. CANTILLY VILLENOY	Verghot	
Sept 3d VILLENOY	Section of D in action - Bivouac.	
	No fighting Crossed R. MARNE at GERMIGNY	

D I A R Y
or
…E SUMMARY (Vide F.S.Regns:)

Hour, Date, Place.	Summary of Events and Information	Remarks and references to Appemdices
Sept 5th CHAILLY en BRIE	Retired from MONTBISE CHATEAU through Bois de JOUARRE. E Battery in action at LE FAYET S of Bois de DON E against DOUE. Heavily shelled by Germans: no casualties – Several casualties from shell fire to Germans reported by A.G. Cavalry –	
Sept. 6th ~~CHAILLY en BRIE~~ VILBERT	Retired from CHAILLY S W across difficult ravine at DESBORDES through FORET de MALVOISINE & Bois de DOTIGNY to VILBERT. No firing.	
	Advance began	
Sept. 7th PEZARCHES	Marched from VILBERT & assembled under cover N.E corner of Bois de DOTIGNY. Advanced in the afternoon to PEZARCHES. Enemy holding entrance to Bois de MALVOISINE. D. Group sent forward with one gun & shelled wood at 1000yds. Remaining batteries in action S. of PEZARCHES. Germans finally retired. Billets at PEZARCHES	

I A R Y

ARY (Vide F.S.Regns:)

Hour, Date, Place.	Summary of Events and Information	Remarks and references to Appemdices
Sept. 8th LES POTEES	Marched from PELARCHES to CHAILLY. 1st Cavalry bde. in action S of COULOMMIERS, when near CHAILLY en BRIE Batteries were shelled from the N. Both Batteries in action - fired some rounds. Advance continued. Several small bodies of Germans seen towards DOUE. Went into billets in the dark in LES POTEES	
Sept. 9th l'HOTEL ½ mile S of LE GRAND GLAIRET	Marched N from LES POTEES to DOUE. Then to MAUROY. Batteries in action against Germans moving N & E of JOUARRE. D Battery & 1st Pl[illegible] Section of E heavily shelled in an exposed position. Major Gillson wounded. Lt Parker who was with a single gun in advance killed. Lt Googh killed shortly after. Major Gillson was wounded. A shell went through shield of E Battery's section & killed layer. Remaining guns E Battery brought into action & were heavily shelled.	1 gunner killed 8 wounded. Lts Googh & Parker were buried in the evening, at the farm l'HOTEL ½ mile S. of LES GRANDS GLAIRETS
Sept. 10th ROUGEVILLE	Marched from l'Hotel Dieu to Chateau PERREUSE. Remained there under cover, watching large columns of enemy marching W to E, N of R. MARNE - marched in the afternoon to ROUGEVILLE preparatory to crossing The MARNE	

D I A R Y
or
SUMMARY (Vide F.S. Regns:)

Hour, Date, Place.	Summary of Events and Information	Remarks and references to Appemdices
Sept 11th PASSY	Crossed River. MARNE at MIRY, & advanced N. When S. of BRUYETZ saw several columns of Germans retiring N of BRUYETZ. Range too long. D Maxwell with advance guard shelled columns. Good deal of confusion through not knowing which were our own troops or enemy. 5th Cav Brigade captured baggage & prisoners.	
Sept 12th TIGNY	Brigade marched from PASSY. Large columns seen from BLANZY moving towards SOISSONS. Supposed to be French - later discovered to be Germans. E Battery in action in the evening to assist French advance on SOISSONS. Very wet - billets TIGNY in the evening. Going very bad	
Sept 13th CHASSEMY	Marched from TIGNY to seize crossings of R. AISNE. Were opposed by GERMANS after MONT de SOISSONS FERME. D in action against R. VESLE Bridge. 1 mile N of CIRY. In action on high ground N E of CHASSEMY. Batteries recalled to engage German infantry in rear. About 100 prisoners taken & 70 ~~[illegible]~~	

R DIARY
or
…ENCE SUMMARY (Vide F.S.Regns:)

Hour, Date, Place.	Summary of Events and Information	Remarks and references to Appemdices
Sept 14th CHASSEMY	Brigade moved out of CHASSEMY to a covered position - 18 pr battery shelled by Germans 400 yds S. of CHASSEMY & 3 guns destroyed. Batteries returned to billets in the evening -	
Sept 15th DIMÉ.	Batteries moved from billets at CHASSEMY to CHATEAU - were unable to cross Bridge at VAILLY & were shelled retiring 4 men wounded - 3 horses killed - Germans were using howitzers: fire very accurate. A. C. was shelled in CHASSEMY & lost 20 horses. 1 man killed 3 wounded	
Sept 16th DIMÉ.	Batteries in action on the S of R. AISNE, near CHASSEMY. D Battery fired a few rounds at long range to support inf attack on CONDE BRIDGE. Returned in the evening to DIMÉ.	

A R Y

INT... Y (Vide F.S.Regns:)

Hour, Date, Place.	Summary of Events and Information	Remarks and references to Appemdices
Sept 17th DIMÉ	Both Batteries moved forward to a position of readiness S. of CHASSIGNY, to assist Brigade of infantry at CONDÉ. D fired a few rounds but the range was very long. Returned to DIMÉ. Very bad weather. The Cav. Division was reorganised at DIMÉ & one battery was attached to each Brigade D to 3rd Cav. Brigade E " 5th " " The headquarters were attached to 2nd Cav Divn. Headquarters –	
Sept 18th BRAINE	Headquarters moved to DIMÉ	This diary is incomplete as all the baggage of the Brigade was lost Aug 25th & did not rejoin until Sept. 15th. It contained all the stationery of the Brigade. J A Barrell Capt Adj

Hour, Date, Place.	Summary of Events and Information	Remarks and references to Appendices
	HQ. R.H.A. 2nd Cav. Divn	
Sept 19th ~~1914~~ BRAINE	Brigade was split up on 18th. D. Battery attached to 3rd Bde, Cav. E " " " 5th " Cav. HQ & AC to 2nd Cav Div HQ. The battle along R AISNE continues. The 2nd Cav Divn is attached to General Reserve & remains in its present billets	This War Diary now refers only to HQ. Royal Horse Artillery 2nd Cav. Divn
Sept 20th BRAINE	Battle on R AISNE continues. 2nd Cav Divn remains in billets. Weather very wet & cold.	
Sept 21st BRAINE	Battle on R AISNE continues. 2nd Cav. Divn remains in billets. Weather very wet & cold.	

Hour, Date, Place.	Summary of Events and Information.	Remarks and references to Appemdices
Sep. 22 BRAINE	2nd Cav. Divn. still in billets at BRAINE. No news of what is going on in front. Weather cold & stormy. Col. Brooks received orders to join 15 Brigade R.F.A. but on enquiry at 2nd Corps Headquarters nothing was known of his being required.	App. I. Copy of a German Officers letter. recd. 22.9.14
Sept. 23rd BRAINE	Headquarters R.A. 2nd Cav. Div. was broken up. Col. Brooks being sent to V. Division, & personnel returned to Batteries	

J.A. [illegible] Capt.
Adjt. 3rd Bde
RHA

BEF

2 CAV DIV TROOPS

3 Bde RHA
AMMO COL

1914 AUG + 1918 FEB

1st Cavalry Divisional Artillery.

Became 2nd CAVALRY DIVISIONAL AMMUNITION COLUMN 16.10.14.

3rd BRIGADE R. H. A.

AMMUNITION COLUMN

5th AUGUST to 12th OCTOBER 1914.

Instructions regarding War Diaries and Intelligence Summaries are contained in F. S. Regs., Part II. and the Staff Manual respectively. Title pages will be prepared in manuscript.

WAR DIARY

or

~~INTELLIGENCE SUMMARY.~~

(Erase heading not required.)

23 C.R.A.C. Army Form C. 2118.

Hour, Date, Place	Summary of Events and Information	Remarks and references to Appendices
Aldershot 7 a.m. 5-8-14	Captain Parsons and two storemen joined. Drew Equipment	
6-8-14 7 PM all day	Personnel and 26 horses joined from 'C' Bty. sorted equipment, and organised Subsections.	
7-8-14 all day 11 PM	sorted equipment issued and marked ditto Balance of horses joined from Remount depot at Aldershot.	
8-8-14 all day	Teamed horses, fitted harness: fitted stores shoes.	
9-8-14 all day	ditto	
10-8-14	Marching order	

Instructions regarding War Diaries and Intelligence Summaries are contained in F. S. Regs., Part II. and the Staff Manual respectively. Title pages will be prepared in manuscript.

WAR DIARY
or
INTELLIGENCE SUMMARY.
(Erase heading not required.)

Army Form C. 2118.

Hour, Date, Place	Summary of Events and Information	Remarks and references to Appendices
11-8-14	Marching order parade reported ready	
(12-13-14) 8-14	completed as required	
15-8-14	Entrained in 4 trainloads with J Battery for Southampton	
16-8-14	Sailed at 11 a.m. with 2 trainloads only	
17-8-14	Arrived ROUEN 11 a.m. disembarked from 2 till 7.30 into camp at [illegible] BRUYERES	
18-8-14	Other two trainloads joined	
19-8-14		

Instructions regarding War Diaries and Intelligence Summaries are contained in F. S. Regs., Part II. and the Staff Manual respectively. Title pages will be prepared in manuscript.

WAR DIARY
or
INTELLIGENCE SUMMARY.
(Erase heading not required.)

Army Form C. 2118.

Hour, Date, Place	Summary of Events and Information	Remarks and references to Appendices
20-8-14	Marched to station 1.30. entrained between 3 and 5 – started 6.53 PM	
21-8-14	JEUMONT 7 a.m. detrained by 8.20 a.m. joined 5th Cav Bde. moved at noon via MERBES-LE-CHATEAU to billets at MERBES ST-MARIE at 7 P.M	Impossible to keep orders. Many are verbal, some come to the Officer i/c Column and transport. Others have to be passed on.
22-8-14	Stood to arms 4.30 a.m	
7.15	moved to PEISSANT	
1.45	" ROUVEROY	
6.30	To billets at CROIX LES ROUVEROY	
23-8-14 4 a.m.	Ready to move	
8 a.m.	To near GRAND RENG	
4.30 pm	To sugar factory S W of GIVRY	
	Parked for night.	

3

Army Form C. 2118.

Instructions regarding War Diaries and Intelligence Summaries are contained in F. S. Regs., Part II. and the Staff Manual respectively. Title pages will be prepared in manuscript.

WAR DIARY
or
INTELLIGENCE SUMMARY.
(Erase heading not required.)

Hour, Date, Place	Summary of Events and Information	Remarks and references to Appendices
24-8-14 5 a.m	To HAUDMONT	
	Arrived 10 a.m parked	
25-8-14 8 a.m	marched via BACCHANT to TAISNIERES	
2.30 PM	Arrived and camped	
9.30 AM	Saddled up in readiness	
26-8-14 4 a.m	via GRAND PRET to BARZY	
	parked at BARZY	
4.30 PM	orders to move to HAMMAPPES	
7.30 PM	arrived HAMMAPPES ~~parked~~ camped	
27-8-14 5.30	Stood to arms	
12 noon	marched via GUISE and MONT DORIGNY	
	to LUCY, parked on road at 10 PM	

(9 26 6) W 257—976 100,000 4/12 H W V 79/3298

Instructions regarding War Diaries and Intelligence Summaries are contained in F. S. Regs., Part II. and the Staff Manual respectively. Title pages will be prepared in manuscript.

WAR DIARY
or
INTELLIGENCE SUMMARY.
(Erase heading not required.)

Army Form C. 2118.

Hour, Date, Place	Summary of Events and Information	Remarks and references to Appendices
28-8-14	Stood to arms 12 30 a.m	
4.30 am	marched via LA FERE to SINCENY	
2. PM	arrived SINCENY parked for 2 hours and took harness off. having had harness on for 34 hours. and having marched 43 miles in the last 26 hours.	
5 30 PM	On to camp at PIERREMONDE.	
29-8-14. morning	Refitted J Battery R H A and refilled cavalry with S.A.A Replenished from Ammunition Park	
8.30 PM	Ready to move.	
10.45 PM	Marched toward St BANDRY	

(9 26 6) W 257—976 100,000 4/12 H W V 79/3298

Instructions regarding War Diaries and Intelligence Summaries are contained in F. S. Regs., Part II. and the Staff Manual respectively. Title pages will be prepared in manuscript.

WAR DIARY
or
INTELLIGENCE SUMMARY.
(Erase heading not required.)

Army Form C. 2118.

Hour, Date, Place	Summary of Events and Information	Remarks and references to Appendices
30-8-14 10 AM	Reached ST BANDRY after a 25 mile night march.	AMBLENY.
	Parked and went into camp at 6 PM	
31-8-14 noon	Marched to camp at St PIERRE AIGLE	
midnight	marched with transport via VERTE FEUILLE VILLERS-COTTERETS and parked at	
1-9-14 8 am	COYOLLES	
4 PM.	marched to LA VILLENEUVE SOUS THURY getting clear with great difficulty.*	*orders to move were delayed, and a road shown as good by map, proved impassable. Got mixed up with rear guard, ~~and~~ in forest.
9.30 PM	marched via MAREUIL to	
2-9-14 10 am	MEAUX	

Instructions regarding War Diaries and Intelligence Summaries are contained in F. S. Regs., Part II. and the Staff Manual respectively. Title pages will be prepared in manuscript.

WAR DIARY
or
INTELLIGENCE SUMMARY.
(Erase heading not required.)

Army Form C. 2118.

Hour, Date, Place	Summary of Events and Information	Remarks and references to Appendices
2-9-14 6 PM	Billets at TRILPORT with 5th Cav Bde	
8 "	reached billets	
3-9-14 3.30 am	marched with transport to AULNOY	
9.30 "	parked AULNOY.	
4-9-14 3.30 PM	with transport to St PIERRE EN VEUVE	
10. PM	marched towards MELUN	↑ end of retirement. Battery and Regiments used little Amn., and were always filled up in camp at night even arriving for any during the day. Consequently Amn Col was always well behind with transport, and was only once in very serious difficulty.
5-9-14 3 AM	parked at NESLES	
1.15 PM	marched to camp at SEGRES via ROZOY, and BERNAY, with HQ for the night	
6-9-14 8. a m	To CHATEAU DE LUMIGNY with Brigade. Bivouacked 7 PM.	

Army Form C. 2118.

Instructions regarding War Diaries and Intelligence Summaries are contained in F. S. Regs., Part II. and the Staff Manual respectively. Title pages will be prepared in manuscript.

WAR DIARY

or

INTELLIGENCE SUMMARY.

(Erase heading not required.)

Hour, Date, Place		Summary of Events and Information	Remarks and references to Appendices
7-9-14	5.30 am.	Stood ready to move.	Advance commenced. CAVALRY ahead, Cavy Am. Col. and transport behind infantry fighting troops – could not get up to own Bde in their billets.
	11 am	moved via CHAILLY and bivouacked at CHAUFFRY at 10 PM.	
8-9-14	4 am	To REBAIS	
	6.30 am	To GIBRALTAR – shelled slightly	→ Tried putting transport and Am Col up in front of infantry in the advance. Result got in the way.
	6 PM	To bivouac with Brigade at BOULVILLIERS. Refilled J Battery.	
9-9-14	8.am	To CHARLY SUR MARNE; bivouacked at 9 PM.	
10.9.14	6 am	Parked between CHARLY and CROUTTES.	→ Kept back again behind infantry.
	9 PM	To billet at PASSY with Brigade	
11-9-14		To PARCY TIGNY billets with Brigade.	
12-9-14		To MONT de SOISSON FARM	
13-9-14		To BRAINE	

Instructions regarding War Diaries and Intelligence Summaries are contained in F. S. Regs., Part II. and the Staff Manual respectively. Title pages will be prepared in manuscript.

WAR DIARY
or
INTELLIGENCE SUMMARY.

(Erase heading not required.)

Army Form C. 2118.

Hour, Date, Place	Summary of Events and Information	Remarks and references to Appendices
14-9-14 5AM	With J Battery to CHASSEMY; to billets at CERSEUIL. Shelled in CHASSEMY, ~~and~~ spent the day in a covered road; where a GS wagon could not have been turned by any means.	Again pushed on directly behind cavalry, got badly in the way again.
15-9-14	Remained at CERSEUIL	
16-9-14 5am	To VILLERS EN PRAYERE. To join 1st CAV. DIV.	
5PM	To bivouac at BARBONVAL	
17-9-14	BARBONVAL. Detached Lt Meade and 30 N.C.O.'s & 36 horses to form a 'mobile section' to J Battery. Remainder of column joined 7th Bde R.H.A. Am. Col. to form 1st CAV. DIV. AMM. COLUMN	The mobile section system had already been used in 1st CAV DIV to avoid the troubles above mentioned, but we did not see how it worked, as we were stationary till 3rd Oct, and then practically doing a peace march till we joined 2nd DIV again.
18-9-14	BARBONVAL	

Instructions regarding War Diaries and Intelligence Summaries are contained in F. S. Regs., Part II. and the Staff Manual respectively. Title pages will be prepared in manuscript.

Army Form C. 2118.

WAR DIARY
or
INTELLIGENCE SUMMARY.
(Erase heading not required.)

Hour, Date, Place	Summary of Events and Information	Remarks and references to Appendices
19-9-14 — 3-10-14	BARBONVAL. Last two days at BARBONVAL shelling by heavy guns became so near that we went into a wood, and took complete cover from aeroplanes	
29-9-14	H Meade to CAV. DIV. STAFF replaced by LT. SOAMES	
3-10-14	To QUINZY-SOUS-LE-MONT.	
4-10-14	To LE PLESSIER HELEU night march.	
5-10-14	night march to VAUMOISE N of VILLERS COTTERETS	
6-10-14	To ARSY via VERBERIE	
7-10-14	" VILLERS TOURNELLE W of MONDIDIER	
8- "	" LONGPRE NW of AMIENS	
9 "	" BOUQUEMAISON N of DOULLENS	
10 "	" MONCY BRETON NW of CELLERS	
11 "	" BERGUETTE	
12 " (monday)	" via ST VENANT A LA MOTTE	

March 15 / to Oct 12 } 1915 153 / 3/9/15 3rd Bry w RHA. 2 Cav Div

WAR DIARY
or
INTELLIGENCE SUMMARY.

(Erase heading not required.)

Army Form C. 2118.

3.9.15

Place	Date	Hour	Summary of Events and Information	Remarks and references to Appendices
			Page 1. 574	
			Diary of Headquarters IInd Cav Div R.H. Artillery –	
Commenced	15th		March 1915.	
			VIEUX BERQUIN.	
			The original 3rd Bde R.H.A. Comprising D and E Batteries was abolished on the AISNE about the beginning of Sept – Lieut Col BREEKS who was in Command previous to this was appointed a R.H.A. liason Officer and the Adjutant Capt Scarlett took over the duties of Staff Officer R.H.A. 2nd Cav Div. D.R.H.A. remained with the 3rd Cav Bde. E R.H.A joined the 5th Cav Bde and J. R.H.A joined the 4th Cav Bde. These 3 Cav Bdes comprised the 2nd Cav Div which was under the Command of Major General H. de la P. GOUGH	
			This arrangement held good until about 15/3/15 when orders were received that a Headquarters Consisting of a Lieut Colonel, an Adjt, orderly Officer	

Instructions regarding War Diaries and Intelligence Summaries are contained in F. S. Regs., Part II. and the Staff Manual respectively. Title pages will be prepared in manuscript.

WAR DIARY
or
INTELLIGENCE SUMMARY.
(Erase heading not required.)

Army Form C. 2118.

877

Place	Date	Hour	Summary of Events and Information	Remarks and references to Appendices
			Page 4	
VIEUX BERQUIN.				
	March 24th to April 12th		During this period Headquarters remained at VIEUX BERQUIN – D Battery was billeted along the RUE de BOIS, E RHA on the same road closer to VIEUX BERQUIN and J at BLEU. 2nd Cav Div Amm Clm was billeted near Petit Sec Bois and the WARWICKSHIRE Battery RHA which had been attached to the 2nd Cav Div was billeted on the VIEUX Berquin – La MOTTE Road –	
			Organisation of the Staff continued and the Signallers were practised in their various duties under the supervision of the O.C. 2nd Cav Div Signals +	
	April 13th –		The O.C. Warwickshire RHA has received instructions to join the 9th Cav Bde – The transfer of this battery was subsequently delayed owing to an outbreak of measles.	

1577 Wt. W10792/1773 500,000 2/15 D. D. & L. A.D.S.S./Forms/C. 2118.

Instructions regarding War Diaries and Intelligence Summaries are contained in F. S. Regs., Part II. and the Staff Manual respectively. Title pages will be prepared in manuscript.

WAR DIARY
or
INTELLIGENCE SUMMARY.
(Erase heading not required.)

Army Form C. 2118.

Place	Date	Hour	Summary of Events and Information	Remarks and references to Appendices
			Page 3. 876	
VIEUX BERQUIN.	26/3/15		Capt The Hon O. STANLEY joined and took over the Command of 2nd Cav Div Ammunition Column –	
			About this date the remainder of the Headquarter Staff joined and were billeted at VIEUX BERQUIN.	

Composition of Staff

	PERSONNEL Officers	Tptrs	R & File	Total	HORSES Riding	Draught	Total
Lieut - Colonel	1	–	–	1	3	–	3
Adjutant	1	–	–	1	3	–	3
Orderly - Officer	1	–	–	1	2	–	2
Trumpeters	–	1	–	1	1	–	1
Corporals	–	–	2	15(a)	13	–	13
Bombadiers	–	–	2				
Gunners	–	–	11				
Drivers	–	–	5	5	–	9	9
Clerks	–	–	1	1			
Batmen	–	–	6	6			
Total.	3	1	24	31	22	9	31

(a) Comprising Telephone detachment (1 mounted) NCO 2 gunners also 4 signallers 2 orderlies 3 horseholders.

All except the horseholders and Drivers of telephone waggon are trained signallers and telephonists. (Total = 12 signallers).

The Orderly Officer should be trained as a signal Officer.

attached

Armament artificer 1 Staff Sergt –

Instructions regarding War Diaries and Intelligence Summaries are contained in F. S. Regs., Part II. and the Staff Manual respectively. Title pages will be prepared in manuscript.

WAR DIARY
or
INTELLIGENCE SUMMARY.
(Erase heading not required.)

Army Form C. 2118.

825

Place	Date	Hour	Summary of Events and Information	Remarks and references to Appendices
			Page 2.	
			(Cont). And a staff would shortly be reformed —	
			The Brigadier Gen R.H.A. Cav Corps stated that this staff was organised and designed for tactical purposes only —	
			All administrative Correspondence & Control would as before be dealt with by the Brigades to which the Batteries belonged.	
			The Batteries would normally remain with and fight with their Cav Brigades, the Colonel joining the Headquarters 2nd Cav Div —	
			Should it become necessary to Brigade the Batteries they would then come under ~~his~~ tactical Control.	
VIEUX BERQUIN 15/3/15			Lieut Colonel G. GILLSON D.S.O. R.H.A. from England landed at HAVRE.	
19/3/15.			Lieut Colonel GILLSON arrived at VIEUX BERQUIN and joined the Staff of 2nd Cav Div as C.R.A.	
23/3/15			Capt C. J. CLIBBORN R.H.A. from D Battery joined the HQ's 2nd Cav Div as adjutant ~~[illegible]~~ similarly 2 Lieut G.L.A. DUFF from 2nd Cav Div Amm Clm joined as Orderly Officer —	

1577 Wt. W10791/1773 500,000 1/15 D. D. & L. A.D.S.S./Forms/C. 2118.

Instructions regarding War Diaries and Intelligence Summaries are contained in F. S. Regs., Part II. and the Staff Manual respectively. Title pages will be prepared in manuscript.

WAR DIARY or INTELLIGENCE SUMMARY.

(Erase heading not required.)

Army Form C. 2118

Place	Date	Hour	Summary of Events and Information	Remarks and references to Appendices
			Page 5. 878	
VIEUX BERQUIN.				
	April 14th.		A 2nd Cav Div Horse Show took place today organised and run by Capt Alexander 19th H's. A great success. Lieut Col Gillson's Chestnut Gelding won 1st Prize Heavy weight Chargers.	
	April 21st		Orders were received today that the 3 Batteries would be attached to 1st Army and allotted to VII Div.	
	April 22nd		Orders received from VII Div that this Bde will take over the positions occupied by 35th Bde RFA in the vicinity of Laventie. D. RHA to go into action on night of 23rd and E & J Batteries on night 24th.	
	April 23rd		At 10 am orders received for 2nd Cav Div to stand to ready to move at short notice + orders received cancelling our move	

1577 Wt. W10791/1773 500,000 1/15 D. D. & L. A.D.S.S./Forms/C. 2118.

Instructions regarding War Diaries and Intelligence Summaries are contained in F. S. Regs., Part II. and the Staff Manual respectively. Title pages will be prepared in manuscript.

WAR DIARY
or
INTELLIGENCE SUMMARY.
(Erase heading not required.)

Army Form C. 2118.

879

Place	Date	Hour	Summary of Events and Information	Remarks and references to Appendices
			Page 6.	
BOESCHEPE			to join 1st Army – About 11am order for concentration of 2nd Cav Div received + The Division marched to BOESCHEPE and billeted there that night – Very heavy firing heard all day and night in the direction of YPRES. The Germans are reported to have broken through the junction of the French + British line N of YPRES.	
VLAMERTINGHE.	24th April		Orders received for Division to be ready to march at 4am, some units not concentrated till 5am owing to block on roads. Marched to VLAMERTINGHE, through that place and remained halted W of the VLAMERTINGHE – ELVERDINGHE road – At 12 noon orders received that the 3 batteries of the Div were to be lent to the French and support an attack on LIZERNE. Later this order was cancelled – The Division billeted about VLAMERTINGHE.	

1577 Wt. W10791/1773 500,000 1/15 D. D. & L. A.D.S.S./Forms/C. 2118.

Instructions regarding War Diaries and Intelligence Summaries are contained in F. S. Regs., Part II. and the Staff Manual respectively. Title pages will be prepared in manuscript.

WAR DIARY
or
INTELLIGENCE SUMMARY.
(Erase heading not required.)

Army Form C. 2118.

Place	Date	Hour	Summary of Events and Information	Remarks and references to Appendices
			Page 4. 880	
April 25th 1 mile NW of BRIELEN.			At 1pm we received order that the 3 batteries would be detached & were to be lent to the French Commander of the 45th Div – The Batteries were attached to the 90th ZOUAVE Bde Commanded by Lt Col MORDACQ – The Batteries occupied a position along a hedge running roughly N and S just E of the X roads S of ELVERDINGHE along the ELVERDINGHE – BRIELEN road. An advanced HQ with the French Commander was established on the Canal Bank just south of BOESINGHE Station – Under the existing circumstances the Batteries were obliged to occupy their positions in daylight during a French attack and undoubtedly their positions were given away to hostile Aircraft, of whom there were a great many. Before very long the Battery positions were shelled by 6" howitzers and 1 shell fell under the trail of a gun of J Battery, turned it completely over but otherwise did not do	

1577 Wt. W10791/1773 500,000 1/15 D. D. & L. A.D.S.S./Forms/C. 2118.

Instructions regarding War Diaries and Intelligence Summaries are contained in F. S. Regs., Part II. and the Staff Manual respectively. Title pages will be prepared in manuscript.

WAR DIARY
or
INTELLIGENCE SUMMARY.
(Erase heading not required.)

Army Form C. 2118.

Place	Date	Hour	Summary of Events and Information	Remarks and references to Appendices
			Page 8. 881	
April 25th			much damage – In the early morning of the next day I. shifted its Position to a flank –	
			The Bde Head quarters was in a Dug out between D and E Batteries, here there was a telephone exchange with an advanced Hquarters linked up by telephone.	
			About this time the line from the North ran along the Canal to STEENSTRAATE here the Germans held the Bridge and had penetrated as far as the Village of LIZERNE, thence along the Western bank of the Canal to HET SAS here it crossed the Canal again & ran along the Eastern Bank to BOESINGHE from there roughly along the road running SE & S of PILKEM to a point where 5 roads meet South of that place – From this point the line ran to some point near St JULIEN.	
			The French were making great efforts to drive the enemy out of LIZERNE & regain the Bridge heads of Steenstraate and Het Sas. The enemy meanwhile were trying to make a Bridge Head at BOESINGHE. On our immediate front, our objective was to	

Instructions regarding War Diaries and Intelligence Summaries are contained in F. S. Regs., Part II. and the Staff Manual respectively. Title pages will be prepared in manuscript.

WAR DIARY
or
INTELLIGENCE SUMMARY
(Erase heading not required.)

Army Form C. 2118.

Place	Date	Hour	Summary of Events and Information	Remarks and references to Appendices
			Page 9. 862	
1 Mile NW of BRIELEN Square C22 ab.			regain the PILKEM ridge –	
	April 26th		The MOROCCAN Bde attacked today supported by gun fire from English and French batteries – The attack was directed on a point somewhere E of the 5 cross roads S of PILKEM – The attack failed chiefly owing to the employment of gas by the enemy – A further attack to take place at 6.30pm met with a similar result +.	
April 27th –			Today another attack was organised to take place by the Moroccan Bde – The outstanding features of these French attacks seem to be (1) A tremendous bombardment almost entirely by 75's on the front line trenches – this bombardment brings down a hail of heavy shells on all possible Artillery positions by the enemy's heavy howitzers – (2) A feint attack by about 100 men to ascertain what resistance	

Instructions regarding War Diaries and Intelligence Summaries are contained in F. S. Regs., Part II. and the Staff Manual respectively. Title pages will be prepared in manuscript.

WAR DIARY
or
INTELLIGENCE SUMMARY.
(Erase heading not required.)

Army Form C. 2118.

Place	Date	Hour	Summary of Events and Information	Remarks and references to Appendices
			Page 10. 883	
1 Mile NW of BRIELEN.			they are likely to meet with – If this advance is checked the bombardment is repeated with increased intensity – There is no doubt the effect on the German trenches is very marked – (3) During these bombardments the front line trenches are strengthened by the advance of the attacking force. We never actually saw a general attack by the French Infantry though their gun fire was magnificent – The German retort to these French attacks seems chiefly to be machine guns well entrenched assisted by gas cylinders – Once when a portion of the German front line trench was occupied, it was found to contain no Germans, meanwhile the attackers were enfiladed by machine guns and driven out again. The Battery was again shelled at intervals all day.	
28th April			Same procedure same results no appreciable gains on	

1577 Wt. W10791/1773 500,000 1/15 D. D. & L. A.D.S.S./Forms/C. 2118.

Instructions regarding War Diaries and Intelligence Summaries are contained in F. S. Regs., Part II. and the Staff Manual respectively. Title pages will be prepared in manuscript.

WAR DIARY
or
INTELLIGENCE SUMMARY.
(Erase heading not required.)

Army Form C. 2118.

Page 11. 884

Place	Date	Hour	Summary of Events and Information	Remarks and references to Appendices
1 Mile NW of BRIELEN.	28th April (Cont).		either side. There is no doubt the Germans dislike these bombardments this is apparent from the activity displayed by the enemy's aircraft over us and also by constant bombardment of all Artillery positions.	
	29th April		The number of Spies in this area must be enormous. Our telephone wires are continually being cut. People have been caught signalling in rear of us. The French HQ a very obvious house on the Canal bank, in full view of the PILKEM Ridge is never shelled why? All other houses in this area are continually shelled. Too many important orders particularly attack orders are sent perhaps 2 or 3 hours before, down the telephone. I am certain our lines are tapped it is so simple to do so. Orderlies and Officers are continually going to and from these Headquarters yet up to the day of our departure May 1st. The Commandant's house remained intact.	

Instructions regarding War Diaries and Intelligence Summaries are contained in F. S. Regs., Part II. and the Staff Manual respectively. Title pages will be prepared in manuscript.

WAR DIARY
or
INTELLIGENCE SUMMARY.
(Erase heading not required.)

Army Form C. 2118.

Place	Date	Hour	Summary of Events and Information	Remarks and references to Appendices
			Page 12	
April 29th (Cont). 1 Mile NW of BRIELEN.			German aeroplanes continued to circle over us all day, and the usual shelling also took place. Were it not for the regularity of the German shelling I am sure we would have far more casualties. The Brigadier Gen RHA Cav Corps (Gen White Thomson) visited us on a good many occasions during this week when we were under the French.	
April 30th			The usual procedure continued during the day, the intensity of the German fire has increased each day chiefly directed at our support trenches and our Artillery. Up to the present time so far as we could ascertain there was only one heavy battery in this locality. It did sterling work but how could it compete against so many of the enemy's heavy batteries. More heavy batteries are I believe being brought up now. All night the enemies heavy guns fire over us	

Instructions regarding War Diaries and Intelligence Summaries are contained in F. S. Regs., Part II. and the Staff Manual respectively. Title pages will be prepared in manuscript.

WAR DIARY
or
INTELLIGENCE SUMMARY.
(Erase heading not required.)

Army Form C. 2118.

Place	Date	Hour	Summary of Events and Information	Remarks and references to Appendices
			Page 13. 886	
April 30th (Cont) 1 MILE & NW of BRIELEN.			into YPRES and along the YPRES – VLAMERTINGHE Road.	
	May 1st 1915.		May-day – Orders received today from Cav Corps that we are to withdraw when practicable – The house in rear of the HQ dug-out which has constantly been a mark for the enemy's guns probably due to its proximity to the X roads was hit by a 6" shell this morning. It did some damage & wounded 2 or 3 men – Also 2 telephonists in the HQ dugout were hit by pieces of shell. The Colonel decided after consulting B.C's to withdraw by dribblets during daylight – B.C's made their own arrangements for this withdrawal – J Battery went first followed by D then E. D. were shelled while withdrawing their guns from the pits but fortunately the horses were not up – Maj Jelf commanding D was buried by a shell which fell almost against his dugout –	

Instructions regarding War Diaries and Intelligence Summaries are contained in F. S. Regs., Part II. and the Staff Manual respectively. Title pages will be prepared in manuscript.

WAR DIARY
or
INTELLIGENCE SUMMARY.
(Erase heading not required.)

3rd Bde RHA

Army Form C. 2118.

887

Place	Date	Hour	Summary of Events and Information	Remarks and references to Appendices
			Page 14.	
May 1st	1915		Lieut Walrond of the same battery was wounded by the same shell and Lyr Venning very severely wounded - A number of other men were also hit but not very seriously. A 6" shell also fell almost on the HQ dug out more or less burying the 3 occupants and all the instruments in that part of the dug out - By about 1pm all the batteries had withdrawn successfully. Total Casualties 1 officer and about 9 men wounded during the morning - Of these 4 or 5 remained at duty - Great Credit was due to LIEUT SMITH R.A.M.C. who inspired all ranks with his skill and sang froid during a rather trying morning - The CRA communicated his thanks to Colonel MORDACQ the French Commander for his assistance and later wrote to him - Col Mordacq's reply is attached - The 3 batteries billeted in the vicinity of St Jans ter BIEZEN. Bde HQ moved to REMINGHELST.	

Instructions regarding War Diaries and Intelligence Summaries are contained in F. S. Regs., Part II. and the Staff Manual respectively. Title pages will be prepared in manuscript.

WAR DIARY
or
INTELLIGENCE SUMMARY.
(Erase heading not required.)

Army Form C. 2118

888

Place	Date	Hour	Summary of Events and Information	Remarks and references to Appendices
			Page 15 -	
REMINGHELST	May	2nd	Orders received today to rejoin 2nd Cav Div at ESQUELBECQ and form a reserve to the Belgians - Later this order cancelled and the 3rd Battery were put under the orders of the ~~...~~ 1st Army and ordered to March South to Le SART.	
- ditto -	May	3rd	Batteries marched at 7.30 pm to Le Sart - They reached their billets about 1-30 am in pouring rain -	
Le SART.	May	4th	The Bde has been attached to VIII Div - Gen Hussey 4th Corps CRA visited the Batteries this morning. Batteries marched to their waggon lines about 6.30 pm, 1 Section per Battery going into action after dark in order to take over and register	
Rue De Paradis LAVENTIE			The HQ moved into their new billets in the village of LAVENTIE and took over from O.C. 33rd Bde R.F.A. at 8 pm.	

Instructions regarding War Diaries and Intelligence Summaries are contained in F. S. Regs., Part II. and the Staff Manual respectively. Title pages will be prepared in manuscript.

WAR DIARY
or
INTELLIGENCE SUMMARY.
(Erase heading not required.)

Army Form C. 2118.

Place	Date	Hour	Summary of Events and Information	Remarks and references to Appendices
			Page 16 — 884	
Rue de Paradis LAVENTIE.			May 6th. Batteries spent the day registering otherwise nothing of any moment.	
			May 7th A Busy day for everyone preparing for a [illegible] operation which is about to be carried out here.	
			May 8th The attack by 8th Div timed to take place today has been postponed 24 hours.	
			May 9th Bombardment by Batteries of VII & VIII Div's Commenced at 5am [illegible] left. Similarly the Indian Corps attacked on our Right and the 1st & 2nd Div beyond them were also engaged. Some progress was made in the beginning by the 8th Div but it was not supported and practically all the ground gained was lost. The attack could not in any way be considered a success in any way. The Indian made no progress at all. The bombardment	

1577 Wt. W10791/1773 500,000 1/15 D. D. & L. A.D.S.S./Forms/C. 2118.

Instructions regarding War Diaries and Intelligence Summaries are contained in F. S. Regs., Part II. and the Staff Manual respectively. Title pages will be prepared in manuscript.

WAR DIARY
or
INTELLIGENCE SUMMARY
(Erase heading not required.)

Army Form C. 2118.

Place	Date	Hour	Summary of Events and Information	Remarks and references to Appendices
			Page 14. 890	
Laventie.			it would appear was inadequate and our infantry were held up by [illegible] & maxim gun fire. All night there was a heavy bombardment. On our immediate front there was not much activity but a good deal of shelling. Our local communications worked admirably during the day & the following night; there was no hitch or breakdown.	
	May 10th		A further offensive here has been abandoned for the present. The VIIth Div marched South tonight. The French further South seem to have made some progress.	
	May 11th		Intermittent bombardment during the day and night, on our front fairly quiet	
	May 12th		It would appear that everything here is governed by reports & returns — they are legion & ever increasing. Under the circumstances it is almost impossible to do our ordinary work so much time is taken up making up & rendering returns.	

Instructions regarding War Diaries and Intelligence Summaries are contained in F. S. Regs., Part II. and the Staff Manual respectively. Title pages will be prepared in manuscript.

WAR DIARY
or
INTELLIGENCE SUMMARY.
(Erase heading not required.)

Army Form C. 2118.

Place	Date	Hour	Summary of Events and Information	Remarks and references to Appendices
			16. 841	
LAVENTIE	May 13th	1915.	During the night we bombarded on 2 or 3 occasions for short intervals – The first Bombardment was evidently a success as German Very lights were ~~thrown~~ up etc etc, but later these periodic bombardments received little notice from the enemy.	
	May 14th		More bombardments during the night at intervals.	
	May 15th		Nothing unusual	
	May 16th		Heavy firing all night between 11.30pm and 8am. This firing was somewhere in the vicinity of FESTUBERT where the IInd VIIth and Indian Div's attacked.	
	May 17th		Firing again during the night but not on our front.	
	May 18th		Not much firing during the day or night – Pouring rain.	

WAR DIARY
or
INTELLIGENCE SUMMARY.
(Erase heading not required.)

Instructions regarding War Diaries and Intelligence Summaries are contained in F. S. Regs., Part II. and the Staff Manual respectively. Title pages will be prepared in manuscript.

Place	Date	Hour	Summary of Events and Information	Remarks and references to Appendices
			page 19 892	
LAVENTIE	May 19th		All quiet -	
	May 20th & 21st		All quiet -	
	May 22nd		Heavy bombardments S of us, on our front all quiet.	
	May 23rd		Our telephones which worked so well during the operations on 9th May have not worked so well since. Air lines are as a rule not a great success. To be really successful lines must be (1) Buried (2) or laid in a deep narrow trench.	
	May 24th		A strict control is kept on all ammunition we fire in fact no firing is permitted except to repel a determined attack, & German Artillery is daily becoming more active in consequence as we are unable to retaliate.	
	May 25th		Heavy firing during night of 24th.	

1577 Wt. W10791/1773 500,000 1/15 D. D. & L. A.D.S.S./Forms/C. 2118.

Army Form C. 2118.

Instructions regarding War Diaries and Intelligence Summaries are contained in F. S. Regs., Part II. and the Staff Manual respectively. Title pages will be prepared in manuscript.

WAR DIARY
or
INTELLIGENCE SUMMARY.
(Erase heading not required.)

893

Place	Date	Hour	Summary of Events and Information	Remarks and references to Appendices
			Page 20	
LAVENTIE	May 26th		Our dressing station shelled fortunately no direct hits. Shelling during the day on our front increased observation evidently from a Captive balloon.	
	May 27th		Usual shelling by the enemy no reply from us:-	
	May 28th		A quiet day and night	
	May 29th - 30th		All quiet.	
	May 31st		Orders received that the 5th Bde RHA is to be withdrawn from action at once and join Cav Div at LE NIEPPE. Handed over to OC V th Bde RHA at 10 pm and marched through La GORGUE - MERVILLE HAZEBROUCK to our new billeting area.	
	June 1st		to Sept 3rd Batteries have been out of action during this period chiefly through the shortage of ammunition:- In July and August H.E. to up to 50% has been issued and is now carried.	

1977 Wt. W10793/1773 500,000 3/15 D. D. & L. A.D.S.S./Forms/C. 2118.

Instructions regarding War Diaries and Intelligence Summaries are contained in F. S. Regs., Part II. and the Staff Manual respectively. Title Pages will be prepared in manuscript.

1915

WAR DIARY
or
~~INTELLIGENCE SUMMARY~~
(Erase heading not required.)

3rd Brigade R. H. A.

Army Form C. 2118

Place	Date	Hour	Summary of Events and Information	Remarks and references to Appendices
NORRENT	Oct	12th - 16th	- NIL -	
	Oct	17th	The Brigade moved to old billets in the ROQUETOIRE area	
	"	18th	- NIL -	
	"	19th	Orders received to march to THIEMBRONNE.	
	"	20th	2nd Cavalry Division moved into winter quarters	
			D Battery went to LINGHEM	
			E " " " HOLQUELIERS.	
			T. " " " AVROULT	
			Ammunition Column " " MERCK.	
	Oct	21st - 23rd	- NIL -	

1875 Wt. W593/826 1,000,000 4/15 J.B.C. & A. A.D.S.S./Forms/C. 2118.

Instructions regarding War Diaries and Intelligence Summaries are contained in F. S. Regs., Part II. and the Staff Manual respectively. Title Pages will be prepared in manuscript.

WAR DIARY
or
~~INTELLIGENCE SUMMARY~~
(Erase heading not required.)

3rd Bde R. H. A.

Army Form C. 2118

Place	Date	Hour	Summary of Events and Information	Remarks and references to Appendices
THIEMBRONNE	Oct 24th – Nov 26th		During the whole of this period the batteries were making preparations for winter training. N.C.O's were called for to go as instructors to Kitcheners Army and were to be trained as instructors before sent. A number of young officers from R.M.A Woolwich were attached to the Brigade for a course of instruction. Meanwhile all captains & all subalterns of more than 3 years service were to be posted to R.F.A. Of these Capt C.T. Clibborn was posted to 23rd Div Arty (as Brigade Major) Capt. SOAMES to 14th Division (to Command a battery) Capt IVALWYN to England (to Command a battery) Capt M.H. DENDY to 7th Division (as G.S.O 3.)	

1875 Wt. W593/826 1,000,000 4/15 J.B.C. & A. A.D.S.S./Forms/C. 2118.

Instructions regarding War Diaries and Intelligence Summaries are contained in F. S. Regs., Part II. and the Staff Manual respectively. Title Pages will be prepared in manuscript.

WAR DIARY
or
~~INTELLIGENCE SUMMARY~~
(Erase heading not required.)

3rd Bde R.H.A.

Army Form C. 2118

Place	Date	Hour	Summary of Events and Information	Remarks and references to Appendices
THIENBRONNE	Oct 24th – Nov 26th (Contd).			
			Lieut V. WALROND was posted to 2nd Division	
			" T.R. ANDERSON " " MEERUT Division.	
			The following officers arrived.	
			2nd Lieut T.S. FULLER R.F.A. attached to HQ Qrs.	
			" K.A. TOWNSEND " " " D R.H.A.	
			" M.N. DEWING " " " E R.H.A.	
			" L.W. CUNIS " " " E R.H.A.	
			" N.G. PRING " " " I R.H.A.	
			" C.T.L. LUTYENS " " " I R.H.A.	
			Lieut H.H. MASSY " " " I R.H.A.	
			2nd Lieut R. COCHRANE " " Amm Col.	
			J.W.A. WILKES " " "	

1875 Wt. W593/826 1,000,000 4/15 J.B.C. & A. A.D.S.S./Forms/C. 2118.

Instructions regarding War Diaries and Intelligence Summaries are contained in F. S. Regs., Part II. and the Staff Manual respectively. Title Pages will be prepared in manuscript.

WAR DIARY or ~~INTELLIGENCE SUMMARY~~ 3rd Brigade R. H. A

(Erase heading not required.)

Army Form C. 2118

Place	Date	Hour	Summary of Events and Information	Remarks and references to Appendices
THIEMBRONNE	Nov 27th		Orders received to the effect that the Brigade would be attached to the 11th Corps, 1st Army.	
	Nov 28th		Colonel OLLIVANT and Battery Commanders motored to XIth Corps Headquarters in MERVILLE and were conducted round the proposed new positions.	
	Nov 29th		Brigade Headquarters moved to INGHEM 'D' Battery remained at REMILLY WIRQUIN E Battery and a section of the Ammunition Column moved to ECQUES. 'J' Batty moved to INGHEM. The remainder of the Ammunition Column less S.A. Section, which remained at MERCK moved to HERBELLE	
	Nov 30th		The Brigade less E Batty & section of Amm. Col marched via THEROUANNE - AIRE - ST VENANT - MERVILLE to FOSSE - arriving at their wagon lines at 7 p.m.	

Instructions regarding War Diaries and Intelligence Summaries are contained in F. S. Regs., Part II. and the Staff Manual respectively. Title Pages will be prepared in manuscript.

WAR DIARY 3rd Bde R.H.A

or

~~INTELLIGENCE SUMMARY~~

(Erase heading not required.)

Army Form C. 2118

Place	Date	Hour	Summary of Events and Information	Remarks and references to Appendices
	Nov.	30th.	Brigade Headquarters went to LACOUTURE. D & J Batteries with their section of the Ammunition Column are now attached to the 46th (N.M) Division. E Battery to the 7th Division.	
LACOUTURE.	Dec	1st	One section of D Battery went in to action in the evening in a position 800 yards N.N.W. of ROUGE CROIX (S. of NEUVE CHAPELLE)	
	Dec	2nd	~~J. Battery went into action in the evening in a position~~ The remainder of D. Battery joined the ~~other~~ section in action in the evening.	
	Dec	3rd	Colonel OLLIVANT went to BOUT DE VILLE to command the left Group of the 46th Division whilst Colonel LEVESON GOWER was on leave. J. Battery went in to action in a position just off the LACOUTURE – RICHBOURG – St VAAST road 800 yards S.W of RICHBOURG Church.	

Instructions regarding War Diaries and Intelligence Summaries are contained in F. S. Regs., Part II. and the Staff Manual respectively. Title Pages will be prepared in manuscript.

WAR DIARY
or
~~INTELLIGENCE SUMMARY~~
(Erase heading not required.)

3rd Bde R.H.A

Army Form C. 2118

Place	Date	Hour	Summary of Events and Information	Remarks and references to Appendices
LACOUTURE.	Dec ~~3rd~~ Continued.		46th Division received orders to withdraw. They are to be relieved by the 19th Division & relief are to be completed by 5 p.m. tomorrow.	
	Dec. 4th.		Colonel OLLIVANT handed over command of the Left Group and when riding ~~[illegible]~~ back ~~from~~ to LACOUTURE, a telephone wire caught up in his mouth breaking his upper jaw. The telephone wires all over the country are a great source of danger, as in many places they are stretched loosely across the road just low enough to cause severe injuries to anyone coming along on a horse ~~[illegible]~~.	
	~~Dec~~	~~5th~~	~~[illegible]~~ owing to change of Division. There was considerable difficulty	

1875 Wt. W593/826 1,000,000 4/15 J.B.C. & A. A.D.S.S./Forms/C. 2118.

Instructions regarding War Diaries and Intelligence Summaries are contained in F. S. Regs., Part II. and the Staff Manual respectively. Title Pages will be prepared in manuscript.

WAR DIARY

or

~~INTELLIGENCE SUMMARY~~

(Erase heading not required.)

3rd Bde R. H. A.

Army Form C. 2118

Place	Date	Hour	Summary of Events and Information	Remarks and references to Appendices
LACOUTURE	Dec 5th		~~for some days in getting supplies & ordnance stores~~ [illegible] ~~or materials for horse standings which were non existent~~ [illegible] ~~in the wagon lines allotted to 3rd Bde RHA.~~ [illegible]	ESW
	Dec 6th – 8th		— NIL —	
	Dec 9th		Brigade Headquarters moved to LOCON.	
	Dec 10th – 16th		— NIL —	
LOCON	Dec 17th		G.O.C 2nd Cavalry Division (Major General Sir PHILIP CHETWODE Bart) visited the Brigade accompanied by Colonel FITZGERALD (GSO 1. 2nd Cav. Div). He was conducted round the three Battery positions and the Ammunition Column lines.	

Instructions regarding War Diaries and Intelligence Summaries are contained in F. S. Regs., Part II. and the Staff Manual respectively. Title Pages will be prepared in manuscript.

WAR DIARY or ~~INTELLIGENCE SUMMARY~~

(Erase heading not required.)

3rd Bde RHA

Army Form C. 2118

Place	Date	Hour	Summary of Events and Information	Remarks and references to Appendices
LOCON.	Dec	18th	— NIL —	
	Dec	19th	Brigade Headquarters moved to FOSSE.	
FOSSE	Dec	20th	General BINGHAM (Commanding Cavalry Corps) visited the Brigade, accompanied by Brig. Gen. GILLSON	
	Dec	21st –	23rd – Nil —	
	Dec	24th	Lieutenants B.O. MARSH (S R) and A.O.I BROWNLEE (S.R) joined the Brigade from England. The former was attached to J. Battery & the latter to D. From 5 – 8 pm	
	~~Dec~~	~~24th~~	a heavy bombardment was carried out all along the line calculated to make things as uncomfortable as possible for the enemy not only in the trenches but in billets & on roads behind the trenches.	
	Dec	25th	Every effort was made to prevent a repetition of last years fraternising between the trenches. The German trenches	

1875 Wt. W593/826 1,000,000 4/15 J.B.C. & A. A.D.S.S./Forms/C. 2118.

Army Form C. 2118

Instructions regarding War Diaries and Intelligence Summaries are contained in F. S. Regs., Part II. and the Staff Manual respectively. Title Pages will be prepared in manuscript.

WAR DIARY 3rd Bde R.H.A
or
~~INTELLIGENCE SUMMARY~~

(Erase heading not required.)

Place	Date	Hour	Summary of Events and Information	Remarks and references to Appendices
FOSSE	Dec	25th	were shelled intermittently all day.	
	Dec	26th	'D' Battery's position was heavily shelled by 5.9" from 2.30 - 5 p.m. No casualties resulted but they were forced to withdraw to the wagon line	
	Dec	27th - 29th	- NIL -	
	Dec	29th - 31st	- NIL -	

[illegible]
Lieut Col. R.H.A.
Commdg. 3rd Brigade R.H.A.

1875 Wt. W593/826 1,000,000 4/15 J.B.C. & A. A.D.S.S./Forms/C. 2118.

Vol I

CONFIDENTIAL.

WAR DIARY

of

3rd Brigade. R. H. A.

from: 1st July to 31st July. 1916.

(Volume ~~XXIII.~~).

Instructions regarding War Diaries and Intelligence Summaries are contained in F. S. Regs., Part II. and the Staff Manual respectively. Title Pages will be prepared in manuscript.

WAR DIARY or ~~INTELLIGENCE SUMMARY~~

(Erase heading not required.)

3rd Brigade RHA

Army Form C. 2118

Place	Date	Hour	Summary of Events and Information	Remarks and references to Appendices
HAZEBROUCK	July 1st to 19th		– NIL –	
	20th		Lieut Col J.S. OLLIVANT DSO promoted Temp Brigadier General, left to join 3rd Division	
	21st – 24th		– NIL –	
	25th		Lieut Col T.M. ARCHDALE DSO from 29th Division took over command of the Brigade.	
	26th – 31st		– NIL –	

R.A. Birch Lt
for Lieut Col RHA
Comdg 3rd Bde RHA

1875 Wt. W593/826 1,000,000 4/15 J.B.C. & A. A.D.S.S./Forms/C. 2118.

Vol 2

CONFIDENTIAL.

WAR DIARY OF

H.Q., 3rd BRIGADE, R.H.A.

for August, 1916.

~~VOL XXVI~~

Instructions regarding War Diaries and Intelligence Summaries are contained in F. S. Regs., Part II. and the Staff Manual respectively. Title Pages will be prepared in manuscript.

Army Form C. 2118

WAR DIARY

or

~~INTELLIGENCE SUMMARY~~ 3rd Bde RHA.

(Erase heading not required.)

Place	Date	Hour	Summary of Events and Information	Remarks and references to Appendices
HAZEBROUCK	1/8/16 to 31/8/16		— Nil —	
			1-9-16 T. M. Archdale. Lieut Col RHA Comdg 3rd Bde RHA.	

1875 Wt. W593/826 1,000,000 4/15 J.B.C. & A. A.D.S.S./Forms/C. 2118.

Vol III

SECRET.

WAR DIARY

of

HEADQUARTERS, 3rd BRIGADE R.H.A.

for September, 1916.

VOLUME ~~XXV~~

******

Instructions regarding War Diaries and Intelligence Summaries are contained in F. S. Regs., Part II. and the Staff Manual respectively. Title Pages will be prepared in manuscript.

WAR DIARY 3rd Brigade R. N. A.
~~or~~
~~INTELLIGENCE SUMMARY~~
(Erase heading not required.)

Army Form C. 2118

Place	Date	Hour	Summary of Events and Information	Remarks and references to Appendices
HAZEBROUCK				
	Sept	1st	to 2nd — Nil —	
	Sept	3rd	Orders received that the Brigade would concentrate on 6th inst for march southwards	
	Sept	4th	– 5th — Nil —	
BUSNES	Sept	6th	The Brigade marched via ST VENANT to area BUSNES LAMIQUELLERIE LECORNET BOURDOIS	
SAUTRECOURT	Sept	7th	The Brigade marched via LILLERS to area WAVRANS SAUTRECOURT – CAPENDU FARM.	
VIEIL HESDIN	Sept	8th	The Brigade marched via HUMIERS to area VIEIL HESDIN ST GEORGES – Chau DE FORESTEL.	
	Sept	9th	— Nil —	
REMAISNIL	Sept	10th	Marched to area REMAISNIL – FROHEN-LE-GRAND, a tactical scheme being carried out on the way.	

1875 Wt. W593/826 1,000,000 4/15 J.B.C. & A. A.D.S.S./Forms/C. 2118.

Instructions regarding War Diaries and Intelligence Summaries are contained in F. S. Regs., Part II. and the Staff Manual respectively. Title Pages will be prepared in manuscript.

WAR DIARY 3rd Brigade RHA.

or

~~INTELLIGENCE SUMMARY~~

(Erase heading not required.)

Army Form C. 2118

Place	Date	Hour	Summary of Events and Information	Remarks and references to Appendices
VIGNACOURT	Sept	11th	The Brigade marched via BERNAVILLE and CANAPLES to VIGNACOURT.	
BONNAY	Sept	12th	Marched via BERTANGLES and QUERRIEU to camp North East of BONNAY.	
BONNAY.	Sept	13th	O.C. RHA and Battery Commanders reconnoitred area FRICOURT – MONTAUBAN – LONGUEVAL.	
BONNAY	Sept	14th	"D" Batty RHA moved with 3rd & 5th Cavalry Brigades to Camp North. West of BRAY – SUR – SOMME	
MORLANCOURT	Sept	15th	The Brigade less "D" Battery & "B" Echelon marched to camp North East of MORLANCOURT. On 30 minutes notice to move.	
"	Sept	16th	On 1 hours notice to move.	
	Sept	17th to 30th	Parties sent out periodically to reconnoitre Cavalry tracks to firing line. These ran roughly as follows:– Northern track. North of CARNOY – through NE Boundary of MONTAUBAN – N of DELVILLE WOOD.	

1875 Wt. W593/826 1,000,000 4/15 J.B.C. & A. A.D.S.S./Forms/C. 2118.

Instructions regarding War Diaries and Intelligence Summaries are contained in F. S. Regs., Part II. and the Staff Manual respectively. Title Pages will be prepared in manuscript.

WAR DIARY or ~~INTELLIGENCE SUMMARY~~ 3rd Bde RHA.

(Erase heading not required.)

Army Form C. 2118

Place	Date	Hour	Summary of Events and Information	Remarks and references to Appendices
MORLANCOURT	Sept	17th to 30th	(continued) Southern Track from South of CARNOY – North of MARICOURT – North of BOIS FAVIERE – South of GUILLEMONT – North of BOIS de LEUZE.	
	Sept	30th	The Brigade less D Batty & Heavy Echelon Am Col moved to Camp SW of MEAULTE	
			1–10–16	
			R.A. Hickes Lt for Lieut Col RHA Comdg 3rd Bde RHA.	

1875 Wt. W593/826 1,000,000 4/15 J.B.C. & A. A.D.S.S./Forms/C. 2118.

SECRET.

2 Cav Div.

Vol 4

WAR DIARY

of

H.Q., 3rd BRIGADE, R.H.A.

OCTOBER, 1916.

VOL. ~~XXVI.~~

Instructions regarding War Diaries and Intelligence Summaries are contained in F. S. Regs., Part II. and the Staff Manual respectively. Title pages will be prepared in manuscript.

WAR DIARY ~~or~~ ~~INTELLIGENCE SUMMARY.~~

(*Erase heading not required.*)

3rd Brigade R H A

Army Form C. 2118.

Place	Date	Hour	Summary of Events and Information	Remarks and references to Appendices
	October			
MEAULTE				
	1st to 7th		- NIL -	
	8th		Orders received that the Brigade would be placed at the disposal of the XV Corps and would be attached to the 21st Division.	
	9th		~~Batt~~ The O.C. RHA and battery commanders reconnoitred positions near HIGH WOOD.	
	10th		The Brigade marched out of camp between 9 AM and 11 AM arriving at wagon lines between 3 P.M and 5 P.M. Batteries came into action about 6.30 P.M – 4 gun positions on the plateau S.E of HIGH WOOD, forward section of each Battery in the valley East of HIGH WOOD. Brigade Headquarters were situated in RIFLE TRENCH 400 yards S.E of HIGH WOOD. The zone covered included LE BARQUE and an area 800 yards	

T2134. Wt. W708–776. 500000. 4/15. Sir J. C. & S.

Instructions regarding War Diaries and Intelligence Summaries are contained in F. S. Regs., Part II. and the Staff Manual respectively. Title pages will be prepared in manuscript.

WAR DIARY
or
~~INTELLIGENCE SUMMARY.~~
(Erase heading not required.)

3rd Bde RHA

Army Form C. 2118.

Place	Date	Hour	Summary of Events and Information	Remarks and references to Appendices
400 S.E. of HIGH WOOD	October 10th		broad south of LE BARQUE with the Eastern boundary running through the South Eastern outskirts of that village.	
	11th		The day was spent in Registering. N & X Batteries RHA and D Batt 64th Bde RFA were attached to the Bde forming an RHA Group.	
	12th		30th Division attacked 2.5 P.M. First Objective gained and held in the centre but elsewhere no progress. 2Lt G.P. HEDGES (E Batty) wounded by chance shell on Gun position.	
	13th to 17th		Ordinary day and night firing. The Brigade came under the 12th Divisional Artillery on 14th.	
	18th		30th Division in part of its attacked at 3.40 A.M. The weather was most unfavourable and the assault entirely failed except on the left where slight progress was made in conjunction with the 9th Division. At 7 A.M. the battle dissolved itself into a "joy ride" on the part of the Tanks. At 8.50 A.M. the battlefield was entirely obscured by mist.	

Instructions regarding War Diaries and Intelligence Summaries are contained in F. S. Regs., Part II. and the Staff Manual respectively. Title pages will be prepared in manuscript.

WAR DIARY
or
~~INTELLIGENCE SUMMARY.~~
(*Erase heading not required.*)

3rd Bde RHA.

Army Form C. 2118.

Place	Date	Hour	Summary of Events and Information	Remarks and references to Appendices
400 yards SE of HIGH WOOD	19th		A very hot & cold day. A large number of the dug-outs fell in making the Gun position very uncomfortable	
	20th to 26th		~~[illegible]~~ Ordinary Day and night firing. Most of the time was spent reconnoitring forward positions in the valley East of HIGH WOOD.	
	27th		Orders received that the Bde would rejoin the 2nd Cavalry Division. All positions vacated by 6.30 P.M. The forward Sections were handed over complete to "X" Battery RHA. Night spent in the Wagon Lines between MONTAUBAN and MAMETZ.	
MEAULTE	28th		The Brigade marched to old Camp S. of MEAULTE. D Battery rejoining 3rd Cavalry Brigade.	
	29th to 31st		- Nil -	

T. M. Archdale.
Lt Col RHA
Comdg 3rd Bde RHA.

Vol 5

SECRET.

WAR DIARY

of

HEADQUARTERS, 3rd BRIGADE, ROYAL HORSE ARTILLERY.

NOVEMBER, 1916.

VOL. ~~XXVII.~~ V

Army Form C. 2118.

* Instructions regarding War Diaries and Intelligence Summaries are contained in F. S. Regs., Part II. and the Staff Manual respectively. Title pages will be prepared in manuscript.

WAR DIARY 3rd Brigade RHA.
~~or~~
~~INTELLIGENCE SUMMARY.~~
(*Erase heading not required.*)

Place	~~Date~~	~~Hour~~	Summary of Events and Information	Remarks and references to Appendices
	November			
MEAULTE	1st – 3rd		– Nil –	
	4th		Five Bombardiers from the Brigade sent to 14th Bde RHA at request of 3rd Echelon	
	5th		– Nil –	
	6th		An enemy air raid caused large explosions in a town behind the French lines during the night. The air craft flew over our camp between 9 PM & 11 PM but did not drop any bombs.	
	7th	-	Orders received that the Brigade would march on the 8th for the backward area, and that Batteries would upon their Cavalry Brigade from the time of starting	

Instructions regarding War Diaries and Intelligence Summaries are contained in F. S. Regs., Part II. and the Staff Manual respectively. Title pages will be prepared in manuscript.

WAR DIARY ~~or INTELLIGENCE SUMMARY.~~ 3rd Brigade RHA

(*Erase heading not required.*)

Army Form C. 2118.

Place	~~Date~~ ~~Hour~~	Summary of Events and Information	Remarks and references to Appendices
	November		
BUSSY-LES-DAOURS.	8th	Marched via CORBIE and DAOURS to bivouac west of BUSSY-LES-DAOURS. Weather conditions most unfavourable.	
BELLOY-SUR SOMME	9th	Marched to billets in BELLOY-SUR-SOMME via AMIENS CITADELLE - LONGPRÉ - LA CHAUSSEE. Weather conditions were good.	
GD LAVIERS.	10th	Marched via ABBEVILLE to GRAND LAVIERS and billetted there the night.	
	11th	Marched into ~~[illegible]~~ winter billets which were in villages as follows:-	
		Headquarters RHA — Château 1 mile S.W. of LIGESCOURT.	
		D Batty — NEUVILLE ~~S~~ LES - FOREST - MONTIERS	
		E Batty — WILLEMAN.	

Army Form C. 2118.

WAR DIARY

~~or~~

~~INTELLIGENCE SUMMARY.~~

(*Erase heading not required.*)

3rd Brigade RHA.

'Instructions regarding War Diaries and Intelligence Summaries are contained in F. S. Regs., Part II. and the Staff Manual respectively. Title pages will be prepared in manuscript.

Place	~~Date~~	~~Hour~~	Summary of Events and Information	Remarks and references to Appendices
	November			
LIGESCOURT		11th	(Continued). J. Batty. CAUMONT. Ammn Column PONCHES ESTRUVAL. "D" Battery now came under the Orders of Cavalry Corps to do the work of Depot battery at the RHA School.	
	12th to	15th	– Nil –	
		16th	Headquarters RHA moved to CRECY-GRANGE 1 mile north of CRECY	
		17th	The Ammunition Column moved to ESTREES-LES-CRECY	
	18th	to 26th	This period was spent in making arrangements for winter training	

J. W. Hailey Lt for Lt Col RHA
Commdg 3rd Bde RHA.

CONFIDENTIAL.

Vol 6

W A R D I A R Y

of

HEADQUARTERS, 3rd BRIGADE, ROYAL HORSE ARTILLERY.

DECEMBER, 1916.

VOL. ~~XXVIII~~.

Instructions regarding War Diaries and Intelligence Summaries are contained in F. S. Regs., Part II. and the Staff Manual respectively. Title pages will be prepared in manuscript.

WAR DIARY ~~or INTELLIGENCE SUMMARY.~~ 3rd Bde R.H.A

(*Erase heading not required.*)

Army Form C. 2118.

Place	Date	Hour	Summary of Events and Information	Remarks and references to Appendices
	December 1916			
CRECY - GRANGE.	1st	to 3rd	- NIL -	RAB
	4th		J Battery moved from their billets in CAUMONT to join the 35th Divisional Artillery and went into action in ARRAS.	RAB
	5th	to 19th	- NIL -	RAB
	20th		2nd Lieut R.C. NORTON R.F.A joined E Battery from ENGLAND	RAB
	21st	to 23rd	- NIL -	
	24th		Lieut A.H. HORNBY RHA joined J Battery from the 8th Division	RAB

Instructions regarding War Diaries and Intelligence Summaries are contained in F. S. Regs., Part II. and the Staff Manual respectively. Title pages will be prepared in manuscript.

WAR DIARY ~~or INTELLIGENCE SUMMARY.~~

3rd Bde RHA

(*Erase heading not required.*)

Army Form C. 2118.

Place	Date	Hour	Summary of Events and Information	Remarks and references to Appendices
	December 1916			
CRECY – GRANGE	25th & 26th		– NIL –	RAB
	27th		Lieut Colonel A. MELLOR D.S.O. RHA joined to command the Brigade, from the 6th Division	RAB
	28th		Lieut Colonel T. M. ARCHDALE D.S.O. RHA left to join the 16th Division	RAB
	29th to 31st		– NIL –	RAB
			During the whole of this month E Battery remained in billets at WILLEMAN for the purpose of training with cavalry Brigades. D Battery remained at FOREST-MONTIERS as Depôt Battery at the Cavalry Corps RHA school.	RAB

A Mellor
Lieut Colonel RHA
Comdg RHA 2nd Cav Div.

31-12-16

T2134. Wt. W708—776. 500000. 4/15. Sir J. C. & S.

CONFIDENTIAL.

1147

WAR DIARY

of

HEADQUARTERS, 3rd BRIGADE R.H.A.

JANUARY, 1917.

VOL. XXIX.

Army Form C. 2118.

Instructions regarding War Diaries and Intelligence Summaries are contained in F. S. Regs., Part II. and the Staff Manual respectively. Title pages will be prepared in manuscript.

WAR DIARY ~~or~~ ~~INTELLIGENCE SUMMARY.~~ 3rd Brigade R.H.A.

(Erase heading not required.)

Place	Date	Hour	Summary of Events and Information	Remarks and references to Appendices
	January 1917			
CRECY - GRANGE	1st	to 3rd	- NIL -	RAB
	4th		Capt T G DU BUISSON RHA left D Battery to join the 5th Division and command a battery R.F.A.	RAB
	5th	to 9th	- NIL -	RAB
	10th		D & E Batteries changed places, D Battery going into billets at WILLEMAN and E becoming the depot battery at the RHA school at FORET MONTIERS.	
	11th	to 16th	- NIL -	RAB
	17th		2Lieut W. LUCAS, Ammunition Column, evacuated to England sick	RAB

T2134. Wt. W708—776. 500000. 4/15. Sir J. C. & S.

Instructions regarding War Diaries and Intelligence Summaries are contained in F. S. Regs., Part II. and the Staff Manual respectively. Title pages will be prepared in manuscript.

Army Form C. 2118.

WAR DIARY ~~or~~ ~~INTELLIGENCE SUMMARY~~. 3rd Brigade RHA.

(*Erase heading not required.*)

Place	Date	Hour	Summary of Events and Information	Remarks and references to Appendices
	January 1917			
CRECY - GRANGE	18th	to 24th	- NIL -	RAB
	25th		Major W. W. TELF left D Battery to join 30th Division and command a Brigade RFA.	RAB
	26th		2nd Lieut G. DANIA left Ammunition Column to join 34th Division	RAB
	27th	to 31st	- NIL -	RAB

31-1-17

[signature] Lieut Col RHA
Comdg 3rd Bde RHA

T2134. Wt. W708—776. 500000. 4/15. Sir J. C. & S.

CONFIDENTIAL.

WAR DIARY

of

HEADQUARTERS, 3rd BRIGADE, R.H.A.

FEBRUARY, 1917.
VOL. XXX.

===========

Instructions regarding War Diaries and Intelligence Summaries are contained in F. S. Regs., Part II. and the Staff Manual respectively. Title pages will be prepared in manuscript.

WAR DIARY ~~or INTELLIGENCE SUMMARY.~~ 3rd Brigade RHA. HQ

(Erase heading not required.)

Army Form C. 2118.

Place	Date	Hour	Summary of Events and Information	Remarks and references to Appendices
CRECY. GRANGES.	February.			
	1st to 3rd		- Nil -	RAB
	4th.		2nd Lieut A H. JEFFREYS joined the Brigade from 14th Division	RAB
	5th		2nd Lieut K.C. HADOW joined the Brigade from the 12th Division	RAB
	6th to 10th		- Nil .	RAB
	11th		2nd Lieut J. C CURRIE joined the Brigade from the 30th Division	RAB
	12th		- NIL -	RAB
	13th		Major E.F. NORTON RHA joined from Canadian Corps to Command D Battery RHA.	RAB
	13th to 23rd		- NIL -	
	24th.		A party of 3 officers & 27 other ranks from D Battery were sent for a period in action with J. Battery in ARRAS.	RAB

T2134. Wt. W708—776. 500000. 4/15. Sir J. C. & S.

Instructions regarding War Diaries and Intelligence Summaries are contained in F. S. Regs., Part II. and the Staff Manual respectively. Title pages will be prepared in manuscript.

WAR DIARY 3rd Bde RHA.

~~or~~

~~INTELLIGENCE SUMMARY.~~

(*Erase heading not required.*)

Army Form C. 2118.

Place	Date	Hour	Summary of Events and Information	Remarks and references to Appendices
	February			
CRECY GRANGES.	25th to 28th		- Nil -	RAM
			RAMcL Lt for Lt Col RHA. Comdg 3rd Brigade RHA.	

T2134. Wt. W708—776. 500000. 4/15. Sir J. C. & S.

CONFIDENTIAL.

Vol 9

WAR DIARY

of

HEADQUARTERS,
THIRD BRIGADE, ROYAL HORSE ARTILLERY.

MARCH, 1917.

VOL. XXXI.

Instructions regarding War Diaries and Intelligence Summaries are contained in F. S. Regs., Part II. and the Staff Manual respectively. Title pages will be prepared in manuscript.

WAR DIARY ~~or~~ 3rd Brigade RHA.

~~INTELLIGENCE SUMMARY.~~

(Erase heading not required.)

Army Form C. 2118.

Place	Date	Hour	Summary of Events and Information	Remarks and references to Appendices
	March 1917			
CRECY GRANGE	1st.		- Nil -	RAB
	2nd		J Battery returned from the 9th Division to billets at VIRONCHAUX.	RAB
	3rd to 8th		- Nil -	RAB
	9th		Capt H. F. TRIM struck off the strength of the Ammunition Column being evacuated to England sick.	RAB
	10th to 14th		- Nil -	RAB
	15th		Lieut C. H. BORTHWICK joined to Brigade from the 1st Cavalry Division and was posted to the Ammunition Column.	RAB
	16th & 17th		- Nil -	RAB

T2134. Wt. W708—776. 500000. 4/15. Sir J. C. & S.

Army Form C. 2118.

Instructions regarding War Diaries and Intelligence Summaries are contained in F. S. Regs., Part II. and the Staff Manual respectively. Title pages will be prepared in manuscript.

WAR DIARY ~~or~~ ~~INTELLIGENCE~~ SUMMARY. 3rd Brigade RHA

(*Erase heading not required.*)

Place	Date	Hour	Summary of Events and Information	Remarks and references to Appendices
	March 1917			
CRECY GRANGE	18th		A party of 6 N.C.O's and 10 men was sent to the Ammunition Park for work in connection with the preparation of Ammunition Dumps in the forward area.	
	19th	to 20th	- Nil -	
	21st		Capt J. PERRY from the 6th Division assumed command of the Ammunition Column.	
	22nd		- Nil -	
	23rd		Lieut R.H. BAILEY joined from the R.M.A Woolwich and was posted to the Ammunition Column.	
	24th	to 31st	- Nil -	
			31-3-17 [illegible signature] Lieut Col RHA Comdg 3rd Bde RHA.	

T2134. Wt. W708—776. 500000. 4/15. Sir J. C. & S.

CONFIDENTIAL.

G.A. Cav

Vol 10

WAR DIARY

of

HEADQUARTERS, 3rd BRIGADE, R.H.A.

APRIL, 1917.

VOL. XXXII.

Instructions regarding War Diaries and Intelligence Summaries are contained in F. S. Regs., Part II. and the Staff Manual respectively. Title pages will be prepared in manuscript.

WAR DIARY ~~or~~ ~~INTELLIGENCE SUMMARY.~~ 3rd Brigade RHA

(Erase heading not required.)

1R/291

Army Form C. 2118.

Place	Date	Hour	Summary of Events and Information	Remarks and references to Appendices
CRECY - GRANGE	April 1st		- Nil -	RNB
	2nd		Capt A. G. NEVILLE rejoined E Battery from England.	RNB
	3rd		- Nil -	RNB
	4th		Orders received for move to a forward Area.	RNB
	5th		~~The Ammunition~~ The Ammunition Column less Light Echelon subsections marched to BEALCOURT, D & E Batteries to ESTREES LES CRECY. Further move orders for the 6th postponed for 24 hours.	RNB
	6th.		- Nil -	RNB
to WAVANS	7th.		Headquarters moved to WAVANS arriving there 3.30 p.m. D & E. Batteries rejoined the 3rd & 5th Cavalry Brigades respectively at	

T2134. Wt. W708—776. 500000. 4/15. Sir J. C. & S.

Instructions regarding War Diaries and Intelligence Summaries are contained in F. S. Regs., Part II. and the Staff Manual respectively. Title pages will be prepared in manuscript.

WAR DIARY or ~~INTELLIGENCE SUMMARY.~~

(Erase heading not required.)

3rd Brigade RHA

Army Form C. 2118.

Place	Date	Hour	Summary of Events and Information	Remarks and references to Appendices
			the Conclusion of the March.	RAB
HENU	8th		Headquarters and Ammunition Column marched to HENU arriving there about 8 P.M. Light Echelons of Ammunition Column rejoined the Heavy Echelon on the march.	RAB
	9th		The Division now occupied billets in area HENU GAUDIEMPRE PAS WARLENCOURT. A state of readiness at one hours notice to move was ordered. Orders received 8.45 AM. that the Division would march via POMMIER BERLES AU BOIS BRETENCOURT WAILLY RONVILLE thence via the Cavalry Track to a position of assembly S. W. of TILLOY LES MAFFLAINES. Batteries were disposed as follows: A Battery with 3rd Cav Bde, E Batty with 5th Cav. Bde. I Battery under the OC RHA was ordered to march behind the 3rd Cav Bde. The position of assembly was finally reached about 3.30 p.m.	

Instructions regarding War Diaries and Intelligence Summaries are contained in F. S. Regs., Part II. and the Staff Manual respectively. Title pages will be prepared in manuscript.

WAR DIARY ~~or~~ ~~INTELLIGENCE SUMMARY.~~ 3rd Bde RHA

(Erase heading not required.)

Army Form C. 2118.

Place	Date	Hour	Summary of Events and Information	Remarks and references to Appendices
1000x S.W of TILLOY LES MARLAINES	9th (contd)		The light Echelon of the Ammunition Column marched to WAILLY & thence to RONVILLE ~~...~~, the Heavy Echelon staying at HENU. Orders received 7.30 pm that the Division would go back to billets & bivouacs ~~about~~ AGNY and WAILLY.	RAB
"	10th		Roads being very crowded most of the night was spent in marching back to area mentioned above. Orders received 12 noon that the Division would again assemble S.W of TILLOY LES MARLAINES. J Batty marched in rear of 5th Cav Bde but were subsequently placed in rear of the 4th Cav Bde. At 3 Pm 3rd Bde & "D" Batty moved on to position of readiness in the low ground N of NEUVILLE VITASSE, 5th Bde & E Batty to a position of readiness 1000x South of FEUCHY CHAPEL. J Batty with 4th Cav Bde and Headquarters RHA ~~with Divisional Headquarters~~ remained at the position of assembly.	RAB
"	11th.		At 5.30 Am. E Battery & the 5th Cav Bde were heavily shelled and the	

Instructions regarding War Diaries and Intelligence Summaries are contained in F. S. Regs., Part II. and the Staff Manual respectively. Title pages will be prepared in manuscript.

WAR DIARY ~~or INTELLIGENCE SUMMARY.~~ 3rd Bde RHA

(Erase heading not required.)

Army Form C. 2118.

Place	Date	Hour	Summary of Events and Information	Remarks and references to Appendices
TILLOY LES MAFFLAINES 1000x SW	Apr 11th	(Contd)	following casualties were sustained by the battery: wounded 7 men, killed 13 horses, wounded 20 horses.	
			About 9.30 am Batteries were ordered to come into action to support the infantry attack on WANCOURT. The following positions were taken up: D. Batty 1000x N.E ~~[illegible]~~ of NEUVILLE VITASSE.	
			E " 700x South of + roads at FEUCHY CHAPEL.	
			T " 1500x NE of NEUVILLE VITASSE.	
			6 wagons of the Amm^n Col were moved to 800x W. of TILLOY LES MAFFLAINES. Batteries ~~[illegible]~~ had a successful shoot on WANCOURT, D & E catching several parties of enemy in the streets, & T silencing a 77 mm battery on the S.E side of the village. E Batty were subsequently turned on to the ground N E of MONCHY LE PREUX to assist 3rd Cav Div in the village. At 6 pm under cover of a heavy snow storm Batteries were withdrawn and followed the remainder of the Division to bivouacs in the WAILLY AGNY area.	RKH.

T2134. Wt. W708—776. 500000. 4/15. Sir J. C. & S.

Army Form C. 2118.

Instructions regarding War Diaries and Intelligence Summaries are contained in F. S. Regs., Part II. and the Staff Manual respectively. Title pages will be prepared in manuscript.

WAR DIARY
or
~~INTELLIGENCE~~ SUMMARY.

3rd Brigade RHA

(*Erase heading not required.*)

Place	Hour, Date	Summary of Events and Information	Remarks and references to Appendices
HENU	Apl 12th	The Division returned to the HENU area Headquarters RHA were at HENU arriving there about 9 30 pm.	RAB
"	13th	– Nil –	RAB
"	14th to 18th	– Nil –	RAB
"	19th.	"D" Battery with 3rd Cavalry Bde moved to the FROHEN LE GRAND area.	RAB
"	20th	E Battery with the 5th Cavalry Bde moved to the FROHEN LE GRAND area & were billetted in VILLERS L'HOPITAL. D Batty with their Cavalry Bde moved to the LE BOISLE area & were billetted at BOUFFLERS.	RAB
"	21st to 26th	– Nil –	RAB
"	27th	2nd Lt RH BAILEY left the Ammn Col. to join 50th Div Artillery.	RAB
"	28th to 30th	– Nil –	

[signature]
Lieut Col RHA
Comdg 3rd Bde RHA.

XXI

CONFIDENTIAL.

WAR DIARY

of

HEADQUARTERS, 3rd BRIGADE, R.H.A.

MAY, 1917 - VOL. XXXIII.

Army Form C. 2118.

WAR DIARY ~~or INTELLIGENCE SUMMARY.~~ Headquarters 3rd Bde RHA

(*Erase heading not required.*)

Instructions regarding War Diaries and Intelligence Summaries are contained in F. S. Regs., Part II. and the Staff Manual respectively. Title pages will be prepared in manuscript.

Place	Date	Hour	Summary of Events and Information	Remarks and references to Appendices
	MAY			
HENU	1st to 10th		- Nil. -	RAB
	11th		Orders received that the Division would move to the Fourth Army area.	RAB
	12th		Marched to NAOURS via THIEVRES - MARIEUX - BEAUQUESNE.	RAB
	13th		Marched to AUBIGNY via FLESSELLES - RIVERY - DAOURS. 2nd Lieut G. P. HEDGES joined the Ammunition Column from ENGLAND.	RAB
	14th		Marched to LAMOTTE EN SANTERRE via FOUILLY. 2nd Lieut M. N. DEWING left to join the 3rd Division	RAB
MARQUAIX.	15th		Marched to Bivouacs North of MARQUAIX. E & J Batteries RHA came under the orders of the OC 3rd Brigade RHA on arrival.	RAB
	16th		D Battery RHA joined the remainder of the Brigade at Marquaix.	RAB
	17th & 18th		Spent in Reconnaissance of positions etc to be taken over	
	19th		One section of each battery went into action relieving sections of batteries of the 210th Bde RFA. Positions as follows: D Battery 1500 yards east of LEMPIRE. E Battery 1200 yards SE of RONSSOY J Battery 800 yards N of TEMPLEUX LE GUERRARD	RAB

T2134. Wt. W708—776. 500000. 4/15. Sir J. C. & S.

Instructions regarding War Diaries and Intelligence Summaries are contained in F. S. Regs., Part II. and the Staff Manual respectively. Title pages will be prepared in manuscript.

WAR DIARY ~~or INTELLIGENCE SUMMARY.~~

(*Erase heading not required.*)

Headquarters 3rd Bde RHA

Army Form C. 2118.

Place	Date	Hour	Summary of Events and Information	Remarks and references to Appendices
	May			
ST EMILIE	20th		The remainder of D.E. & J batteries relieved the remainder of the batteries of the 210th Bde RFA. Headquarters moved to ST EMILIE and relieved the Headquarters 210th Bde RFA. The 3rd Brigade RHA with A Batty 296th Bde RFA and D (Howitzer) Batty 210th Bde RFA became the Southern Group of the 2nd Cavalry Division. The zone covered was the ground East of a line from ~~[illegible]~~ TOMBOIS FARM (1500 yards NE of LEMPIRE) to the cross road 1500 yards NNE of HARGICOURT. This line was held by a series of posts by the 4th Cavalry Brigade. The Ammunition Column and Wagon lines remained North of MARQUAIX.	RMB
	21st & 31st		The situation was quiet. No event of any importance occurred.	RMB

31-5-17.

[signature] Lieut Col RHA
Comdg 3rd Brigade RHA.

WO 95/12

CONFIDENTIAL

WAR DIARY

of

HEADQUARTERS 3rd BRIGADE RHA.

from 1st June to 30th June 1917

Volume XXXIV

Instructions regarding War Diaries and Intelligence Summaries are contained in F. S. Regs., Part II. and the Staff Manual respectively. Title pages will be prepared in manuscript.

WAR DIARY ~~or~~ ~~INTELLIGENCE SUMMARY.~~

(*Erase heading not required.*)

Army Form C. 2118.

Headquarters 3rd Bde RHA.

Place	Date	Hour	Summary of Events and Information	Remarks and references to Appendices
ST EMELIE	June			
	1st to 9th		Situation quiet. Nothing of importance to record.	RAB.
	10th		At 2.15 A.m a party of the Royal Scots Greys raided an enemy trench immediately east of GUILLEMONT FARM. The operation was completely successful. 56 Germans being killed and 11 taken prisoner, the most important result being that a division that had only a day or two before arrived from Russia was discovered to be holding the line in front of us. All available guns cooperated and a formidable "box barrage" was brought to bear on the trenches and exits immediately surrounding the objective.	RAB
	11th to 13th		Nothing of importance to record.	RAB

A5834 Wt. W4973/M687 750,000 8/16 D. D. & L. Ltd. Forms/C.2118/13

Instructions regarding War Diaries and Intelligence Summaries are contained in F. S. Regs., Part II. and the Staff Manual respectively. Title pages will be prepared in manuscript.

WAR DIARY
~~or~~
~~INTELLIGENCE SUMMARY.~~
(Erase heading not required.)

Headquarters 3rd Brigade RHA

Army Form C. 2118.

Place	Date	Hour	Summary of Events and Information	Remarks and references to Appendices
ST EMELIE	June 14th.		Major RH SANDERSON RHA ceases to command E Batty RHA having been posted to command a R.A. Depot in England	RHB
	15th to 20th.		Nothing of importance to record.	RHB
	21st/22nd		At midnight after a short bombardment the Germans raided GILLEMONT POST. In spite of a considerable proportion of casualties the garrison put up a very good fight and 12 German dead were left in our lines. Early in the enemy bombardment the S.O.S. rockets were destroyed by a shell with the result that our own barrage was not forthcoming so promptly as it could otherwise have been.	RHB
	23rd to 28th		Nothing of importance to record	RHB

A5834 Wt. W4973/M687 750,000 8/16 D. D. & L. Ltd. Forms/C.2118/13

Instructions regarding War Diaries and Intelligence Summaries are contained in F. S. Regs., Part II. and the Staff Manual respectively. Title pages will be prepared in manuscript.

WAR DIARY or ~~INTELLIGENCE SUMMARY~~.

(*Erase heading not required.*)

Army Form C. 2118.

Headquarters 3rd Brigade RHA.

Place	Date	Hour	Summary of Events and Information	Remarks and references to Appendices
ST EMELIE	June 29th		MAJOR C. T. WALWYN D.S.O. RHA joined from the 3rd Division and assumed command of E Batty RHA	RAB
	30th		Throughout the night an organised shoot was carried out against the roads & tracks leading to the front line as a divisional relief was believed to be taking place.	RAB

R. Miller
Lieut Col RHA
Comdg 3rd Bde RHA

Vol 13

WAR DIARY

of

Headquarters 3rd Brigade R.H.A.

from 1st to 31st July 1917.

Volume No XXXV

I

Instructions regarding War Diaries and Intelligence Summaries are contained in F. S. Regs., Part II. and the Staff Manual respectively. Title pages will be prepared in manuscript.

RH0/1

Army Form C. 2118.

WAR DIARY or ~~INTELLIGENCE~~ SUMMARY.

(Erase heading not required.)

Headquarters 3rd Brigade RHA.

Place	Date	Hour	Summary of Events and Information	Remarks and references to Appendices
	July			
ST EMELIE	1st to 3rd		Nothing of importance to record.	RAB
	4th	12.30 Am	All Batteries cooperated with the Artillery of the 4th Cavalry Division for the occasion of a raid which was carried out by the Inniskilling Dragoons on the enemy trenches and works about COLOGNE FARM.	RAB
	5th to 6th		Nothing of importance to record	RAB
	7th	6Pm	A combined shoot with the Heavy Artillery was carried out on enemy dug-outs and shelters on the BONY HARGICOURT road.	RAB
	8th		One section of each battery was relieved by sections of the 157th Brigade RFA. and was withdrawn to the wagon lines (North of MARQUAIX)	RAB
	9th		The remaining two sections of each battery were relieved and withdrawn to the wagon lines.	

II

Instructions regarding War Diaries and Intelligence Summaries are contained in F. S. Regs., Part II. and the Staff Manual respectively. Title pages will be prepared in manuscript.

WAR DIARY ~~or~~ ~~INTELLIGENCE SUMMARY.~~

(*Erase heading not required.*)

Headquarters 3rd Brigade RHA

Army Form C. 2118.

Place	Date	Hour	Summary of Events and Information	Remarks and references to Appendices
ST EMELIE	July 9th		(Continued) The defence of C Sector was handed over to the 157th Brigade RFA	RAB
MARQUAIX.	10th		Orders received that the Division would shortly be marching to the area about ETREE WAMIN	RAB
	11th		2nd Lieut J. H. MASSEY RFA joined from the 15th Division and was posted to the Ammunition Column	RAB
	12th		E & J Batteries rejoined from Cavalry Brigades and commenced the march north.	RAB
SUZANNE	13th		Marched to Suzanne via CLERY. D Battery rejoined the 3rd Cavalry Brigade	RAB
	14th		Marched to VILLE - SOUS - CORBIE	RAB
	15th		Marched to SARTON	RAB
	16th		Marched to LUCHEUX	RAB

A5834 Wt. W4973/M687 750,000 8/16 D. D. & L. Ltd. Forms/C.2118/13

111

Instructions regarding War Diaries and Intelligence Summaries are contained in F. S. Regs., Part II. and the Staff Manual respectively. Title pages will be prepared in manuscript.

WAR DIARY ~~or~~ ~~INTELLIGENCE~~ SUMMARY.

(Erase heading not required.)

Head quarters 3rd Brigade RHA

Army Form C. 2118.

Place	Date	Hour	Summary of Events and Information	Remarks and references to Appendices
	JULY			
LUCHEUX	17th to 26th		Nothing of importance to record.	RAB
	27th		Orders received that the 3rd Brigade RHA less the Small Arms section of the Ammunition Column would be placed at the disposal of the First Army. The Brigade marched at 12 noon to area North of ST POL.	RAB
	28th		The Brigade marched to the GAUCHIN LEGAL - OLHAIN area	RAB
BETHUNE.	29th		The Brigade marched to wagon lines in the VERQUIGNEUL - LABOURSE - SAILLY LABOURSE area. Brigade Headquarters were established in BETHUNE.	RAB
	30th		Orders were received that batteries would go into action to-night ~~today~~ ~~at~~, E Battery to a position 500 yards west of Fosse No 7 de BETHUNE, D & J Batteries to positions on RUTOIRE Plain. Later this move was postponed till the night of the 1st/2nd August.	RAB
	31st		Nothing of importance to record.	RAB

RABrooke[?] Lt. for Lieut Col RHA Comdg 3rd Bde RHA

2 Cav Div

Confidential

War Diary
of

3rd. Bde. R H A

From 1st August to 31st August 1917

Volume XXXVI

Instructions regarding War Diaries and Intelligence Summaries are contained in F. S. Regs., Part II. and the Staff Manual respectively. Title pages will be prepared in manuscript.

WAR DIARY ~~or~~ ~~INTELLIGENCE~~ ~~SUMMARY~~.

(*Erase heading not required.*)

3rd Brigade RHA

Army Form C. 2118.

Place	Date AUGUST	Hour	Summary of Events and Information	Remarks and references to Appendices
BETHUNE	1st		Nothing of importance to record	RAB
	2nd		Batteries moved into action in the evening in the following positions:-	
			D Battery 400 yards North East of Fosse 7 de BETHUNE on the RUTOIRE PLAIN.	
			E Battery 500 yards North North West of Fosse 7 de BETHUNE	
			J Battery 600 yards South of RUTOIRE FARM on the RUTOIRE PLAIN.	RAB
	3rd		Under orders of the Artillery Group covering the ST ELIE Section of the 46th Division front Batteries assisted in barrage covering a raid on enemy trenches N. W of HULLUCK.	RAB
	4th		- Nil -	RAB
	5th		Batteries remaining in the same positions came under orders of the 2nd Brigade RFA (6th Divisional Artillery) covering the HULLUCH Sector of the 46th Division front.	RAB
	6th		The day was spent in registering.	RAB

Instructions regarding War Diaries and Intelligence Summaries are contained in F. S. Regs., Part II. and the Staff Manual respectively. Title pages will be prepared in manuscript.

WAR DIARY ~~or INTELLIGENCE SUMMARY.~~ 3rd Brigade RHA.

(*Erase heading not required.*)

Army Form C. 2118.

Place	Date August	Hour	Summary of Events and Information	Remarks and references to Appendices
BETHUNE	7th	-	Personnel of Batteries returned to their wagon lines in the LABOURSE - VERQUIGNEUL area, prospective operations having been temporarily suspended owing to unfavourable weather	RAB
	8th to	12th	Nil	RAB
	13th		Batteries returned to their gun positions and assisted in the barrage covering a raid carried out by the 46th Division on the enemy's trenches N.W. of HULLUCH.	RAB
	14th		The day was spent in checking registrations.	RAB
	15th	4 25 Am	The Canadian attack on Hill 70 commenced and Batteries took part in the barrage of the 6th Divisional Artillery. Between 10 + 11 A.m in reply to an S.O.S call from the Canadian Division on our right batteries fired on enemy apparently massing for counter attack North of BOIS HUGO. Throughout the day a number of excellent infantry targets were engaged and a total of over 7000 rounds were fired	RAB

A5834 Wt. W4973/M687 750,000 8/16 D. D. & L. Ltd. Forms/C.2118/13

Instructions regarding War Diaries and Intelligence Summaries are contained in F. S. Regs., Part II. and the Staff Manual respectively. Title pages will be prepared in manuscript.

WAR DIARY 3rd Brigade RHA.
or
~~INTELLIGENCE SUMMARY.~~
(Erase heading not required.)

Army Form C. 2118.

Place	Date	Hour	Summary of Events and Information	Remarks and references to Appendices
	AUGUST			
BETHUNE	16th.		A few infantry targets were engaged with good results	RAB
	~~17th~~	11.45 p.m.	Batteries assisted in the barrage covering a raid by the 5th Leicestershire Regiment on enemy's trenches immediately west of HULLUCH.	RAB
	17th		Orders were received that the Brigade would be withdrawn ~~and~~ would rejoin the 2nd Cavalry Division. Batteries returned to their wagon lines during the night.	RAB
	18th		- Nil -	
	19th		The Brigade marched to the GAUCHIN LEGAL - OLHAIN area and billetted the night there.	RAB
	20th		Brigade marched to FREVENT area. H.d Qrs to GOUEY en TERNOIS. Batteries joined their cavalry Brigades	RAB
	31st		as above.	

[signature] Lt. Col R.H.A.
Comdg 3rd Bde R.H.A.

APPENDIX I to War Diary August

O.C. 3rd Brigade RHA

Copies to
D E & J

Please convey to the batteries under your command my appreciation of and thanks for the admirable support given to my infantry during the time the brigade has been attached to the division, more especially during the execution of raids.

The confidence that my infantry have acquired in the guns of your brigade is sufficient testimony of their sorrow at your departure.

I wish you good luck, in the name of the division, in whatever future task the may be demanded of you.

Wm Thwaites
Major General
Comdg 46th Div.

18 Aug 1917

APPENDIX II to War Diary August 1917.

343

G.O.C.,

2nd Cavalry Division.

No.121 (G.B.), 18th August 1917.

On the departure of D, E and J Batteries R.H.A. from the I Corps, I wish to place on record my grateful appreciation of the excellent work which has been done by them.

These batteries immediately on their arrival in the I Corps area were detailed to support raids over ground which the Brigade and Battery Commanders had very limited opportunities of reconnoitring. The barrages put down by the Horse Artillery were on all occasions very accurate and effective showing that a high standard of gunnery and fire discipline obtains in these batteries.

During the Canadian attack on Hill 70 the Horse Artillery again rendered valuable service, and their fire against the German counter-attacks which were projected across the open in front of the I Corps was most effective.

I would be glad if my thanks could be conveyed to Colonel MELLOR, R.H.A. and the Battery Commanders of D, E and J Batteries.

(Sd) A.HOLLAND Lt.Gen.

Commanding I Corps.

(2)

O.C., 3rd Bde. R.H.A.

For your information.

Lieut. Colonel,

General Staff, 2nd Cavalry Division.

2nd CAVALRY DIVISION
G.S.4848.
19/8/17.
HEADQUARTERS, GENERAL STAFF

Vol 15

CONFIDENTIAL

WAR DIARY

OF

Headquarters 3rd Brigade RHA.

from 1st to 30th September 1917.

(VOLUME XXXVII)

Army Form C. 2118.

WAR DIARY
or
~~INTELLIGENCE SUMMARY.~~
(Erase heading not required.)

3rd Brigade RHA.

Instructions regarding War Diaries and Intelligence Summaries are contained in F. S. Regs., Part II. and the Staff Manual respectively. Title pages will be prepared in manuscript.

Place	Date	Hour	Summary of Events and Information	Remarks and references to Appendices
GOUEY-EN-TERNOIS	1st to 4th September		Nothing of importance to record. Batteries remained in the FREVENT area with their Cavalry Brigades.	RAB
	5th		The Brigade less the S.A.A. Section of the Ammunition Column moved to the area OURTON - BAJUS - LA COMPTE, orders having been received that the brigade would join the 6th Divisional Artillery attached to the First Army.	RAB
	6th		Headquarters and Batteries moved to DROUVIN, Ammunition Column to HESDIGNEUL.	RAB
	7th		At night one section from each battery went into action. Positions occupied were taken over from the 1st Canadian Divisional Artillery and were situated on the S.W. side of the BETHUNE ~~Road~~ - LENS Road about 800 yards S.W. ~~SE~~ of LOOS.	RAB

A5834 Wt. W4973/M687 750,000 8/16 D. D. & L. Ltd. Forms/C.2118/13

Instructions regarding War Diaries and Intelligence Summaries are contained in F. S. Regs., Part II. and the Staff Manual respectively. Title pages will be prepared in manuscript.

WAR DIARY
or
~~INTELLIGENCE~~ SUMMARY.
(Erase heading not required.)

3rd Brigade RHA.

Army Form C. 2118.

Place	Date	Hour	Summary of Events and Information	Remarks and references to Appendices
LOOS.	September 8th		Wagon Lines moved to the area LE BREBIS, BRACQUEMONT and at night the remainder of batteries went in to action in the positions mentioned above. With the addition of ~~the~~ a Section of the 87th (Howitzer) Battery R.F.A. the Brigade now formed the group covering the left battalion of the Right Brigade of the 6th Division	RAB
	8th to 11th.		This period was spent in registering. ~~The~~ The zone covered by the Group had a breadth of about 900 yards with the BOIS DIX-HUIT in the centre.	RAB
	12th		During the shelling of LE BREBIS by a 15 cm gun a stable in E Battery's wagon line was hit and by one shell 3 men were killed, eight wounded and 25 horses killed, 17 wounded.	
	13th		From 5 P.M to 10 P.M J battery's position was subjected to a hostile destructive shoot but no material damage was done	RAB

A5834 Wt. W4973/M687 750,000 8/16 D. D. & L. Ltd. Forms/C.2118/13

Instructions regarding War Diaries and Intelligence Summaries are contained in F. S. Regs., Part II. and the Staff Manual respectively. Title pages will be prepared in manuscript.

WAR DIARY
or
~~INTELLIGENCE~~ SUMMARY.
(*Erase heading not required.*)

Army Form C. 2118.

3rd Brigade RHA.

Place	Date	Hour	Summary of Events and Information	Remarks and references to Appendices
Loos	14th } 15th }		Nothing of importance to record.	RAB
	16th		Between 4.15 a.m and 6 a.m. the enemy put down an intense artillery barrage on the support trenches of the battalion we covered. This was the northern extension of the barrage which covered ~~...~~ an attempted enemy raid on the Division on our right. All our batteries replied on S.O.S. lines.	RAB
	17th		From 12.30 P.M 4 P.M. J. Battery's position was again subjected to a hostile destruction shoot by 5.9 & 4.2 batteries.	RAB
	18th to 20th		Nothing of importance to record.	RAB
	21st		The enemy carried out a destruction shoot against D Battery with 21 & 15 cm How itzers which lasted from 11 AM to 4 P.M. but no casualties were caused to personnel or guns.	RAB

A5834 Wt. W4973/M687 750,000 8/16 D. D. & L. Ltd. Forms/C.2118/13

Instructions regarding War Diaries and Intelligence Summaries are contained in F. S. Regs., Part II. and the Staff Manual respectively. Title pages will be prepared in manuscript.

WAR DIARY
or
~~INTELLIGENCE SUMMARY~~.
(Erase heading not required.)

3rd Brigade R.H.A.

Army Form C. 2118.

Place	Date	Hour	Summary of Events and Information	Remarks and references to Appendices
LOOS	September 22nd		Nothing of importance to record	RAD
	23rd		From 6 A.M. the Brigade was transferred to the 46th Division for orders and administration. Dispositions remained the same except that the 88th Battery RFA and a Section of the 43rd Howitzer Battery RFA was added to the Group. Their positions were on the South west edge of LOOS village, west of the LOOS CRASSIER. The Group now became the "LOOS RIGHT SUB-GROUP" in support of the 139th Infantry Brigade and the zone covered remained the same with the addition of that of the 88th Battery who covers from FME DE MINES DE LENS to NOGGIN TRENCH.	RAD
	24th		The enemy carried out a heavy bombardment with ~~[illegible]~~ 21, 15 & 10 cm Howitzers of the whole valley from LOOS to LIEVIN which lasted from 5.15 to 7.30 P.M. Batteries were able to get to their dug outs in time & no casualties to guns or personnel resulted except for one gun of D Battery which was slightly damaged.	RAD

A5834 Wt. W4973/M687 750,000 8/16 D. D. & L. Ltd. Forms/C.2118/13

Army Form C. 2118.

Instructions regarding War Diaries and Intelligence Summaries are contained in F. S. Regs., Part II. and the Staff Manual respectively. Title pages will be prepared in manuscript.

WAR DIARY

~~or~~

~~INTELLIGENCE SUMMARY.~~

(Erase heading not required.) 3rd Brigade RHA.

Place	Date	Hour	Summary of Events and Information	Remarks and references to Appendices
Loos	Sept 25th –	31st	Nothing of importance to record	RMB
			During this month the following officers joined the Brigade.	
			Captain E.C.B. DALE RHA to E Battery RHA	
			2Lieut. B.B EDGE RFA to Ammunition Column. 24-9-17	
			2Lieut MURE RFA to " " 29-9-17	
			2nd Lieut J. W. AIRD RFA left to join the 3rd Division	RMB

D Miller
Lieut Col RHA
Comdg 3rd Bde RHA.

WO 95/16

CONFIDENTIAL

WAR DIARY

OF

Headquarters 3rd Brigade R.H.A.

from 1st October to 31st October 1917.

VOLUME XXXVIII

Army Form C. 2118.

Instructions regarding War Diaries and Intelligence Summaries are contained in F. S. Regs., Part II. and the Staff Manual respectively. Title pages will be prepared in manuscript.

WAR DIARY
or
~~INTELLIGENCE SUMMARY~~.
(Erase heading not required.)

3rd Brigade RHA

Place	Date	Hour	Summary of Events and Information	Remarks and references to Appendices
Near LOOS.	October 1st		A 9.30 and 10 PM bursts of intense fire lasting two minutes each were carried out by all batteries on cross roads in rear of the enemys' trenches	RAB
	2nd		Fire as above was repeated at 4.30 AM.	RAB
	3rd		Nothing of importance to record.	RAB
	4th.		A quiet day. At 7.30 P.M simultaneously with a bombardment of our trenches the enemy commenced to search and sweep battery areas and roads about LOOS with 5.9"s & 4.2" howitzers. In reply to the S.O.S. call from the infantry all batteries fired on their S.O.S. lines and fire was kept up at varying rates until 9.30 P.M when the infantry ~~had~~ ~~have~~ reported all quiet. Enemy raiding parties were reported to have attempted to enter our trenches at numerous	

Instructions regarding War Diaries and Intelligence Summaries are contained in F. S. Regs., Part II. and the Staff Manual respectively. Title pages will be prepared in manuscript.

WAR DIARY
or
~~INTELLIGENCE SUMMARY.~~
(Erase heading not required.)

Army Form C. 2118.

3rd Brigade RHA.

Place	Date	Hour	Summary of Events and Information	Remarks and references to Appendices
LOOS	Oct 4th	(Continued)	points on the 46th & 6th Division fronts but only succeeded in one or two isolated places and were everywhere easily repulsed. On this occasion very good work was done by the detachments of all batteries who maintained the required rate of fire throughout under most trying circumstances	RHB
	5th		J Battery's position was shelled almost continuously from 7.30 AM to 12 noon by 5.9" Howitzers. One gun was put out of action but no casualties were inflicted on personnel. After dark one section of J Batty was withdrawn, being relieved by a section of the 464th Batty RFA	RHB
	6th		Orders were received that the Brigade would rejoin the 2nd Cavalry Division. Sections of D and E Batteries were relieved by the remainder of the 464th Battery. The 68th, 97th	

A5834 Wt. W4973/M687 750,000 8/16 D. D. & L. Ltd. Forms/C.2118/13

Instructions regarding War Diaries and Intelligence Summaries are contained in F. S. Regs., Part II. and the Staff Manual respectively. Title pages will be prepared in manuscript.

WAR DIARY
or
~~INTELLIGENCE~~ SUMMARY.

(*Erase heading not required.*)

Army Form C. 2118.

3rd Brigade RHA

Place	Date	Hour	Summary of Events and Information	Remarks and references to Appendices
LOOS.	6th (Continued).		462nd and 464th now became embodied in the group and sections of the D/230 & D/231 Batteries relieved the sections of the 43rd and 87th Batteries respectively. This now became the LOOS Group, covering the whole of the 139th Infantry Brigade and the zone covered had its northern boundary immediately east of CHALK PIT WOOD and its Southern boundary on the northern edge of CITE ST AUGUSTE.	RAB
	7th.		A quiet day. The remainder of D.E. & J Batteries were withdrawn to their wagon lines and at 6 PM the command of the group was handed over to Lieut Col ST JOHN commanding the 14 Army ~~R.H.A.~~ Brigade. RFA.	RAB
BRACQUEMONT	8th.		The move previously ordered was postponed and the Brigade remained ~~was~~ ~~spent~~ in the wagon lines.	RAB

A5834 Wt. W4973/M687 750,000 8/16 D. D. & L. Ltd. Forms/C.2118/13

Instructions regarding War Diaries and Intelligence Summaries are contained in F. S. Regs., Part II. and the Staff Manual respectively. Title pages will be prepared in manuscript.

WAR DIARY
or
~~INTELLIGENCE SUMMARY~~.
(Erase heading not required.)

Headquarters 3rd Brigade RHA.

Army Form C. 2118.

Place	Date	Hour	Summary of Events and Information	Remarks and references to Appendices
BOYAVAL.	Octob 9th		The Brigade marched to billets as under and Batteries rejoined their Cavalry Brigades	
			Headquarters to BOYAVAL	
			D Battery to L'ABBAYE-de-NEUVILLE Farm (3 miles NE of ST POL)	
			E Battery to CHAPELLE ROCOURT 1 mile N of ST POL	
			J. Battery to BERGUENEUSE.	
			Ammunition column to LA THIEVLOYE (5 miles SE of PERNES) where they joined the SAA Section	RAB
	10th to 17th		Nothing to record.	RAB
	18th		Orders were received that the Division would move to an area South of AMIENS.	RAB
HOUVIN HOUVIGNEUL	19th		Brigade Headquarters marched under orders of the 4th Cavalry Brigade to HOUVIN HOUVIGNEUL.	RAB
HAVERNAS	20th		Brigade Headquarters marched to HAVERNAS.	RAB

A5834 Wt. W4973/M687 750,000 8/16 D. D. & L. Ltd. Forms/C.2118/13

Instructions regarding War Diaries and Intelligence Summaries are contained in F. S. Regs., Part II. and the Staff Manual respectively. Title pages will be prepared in manuscript.

Army Form C. 2118.

WAR DIARY
or
~~INTELLIGENCE SUMMARY.~~
(Erase heading not required.)

Headquarters 3rd Brigade RHA

Place	Date	Hour	Summary of Events and Information	Remarks and references to Appendices
HEBECOURT.	October 21st		Brigade Headquarters marched to HEBECOURT (S. of AMIENS) Batteries marched throughout with their Cavalry Brigades and were finally billetted as follows:- D Battery PONT DE METZ E Battery CONTRE J Battery NAMPY The Ammunition Column, who marched with the 3rd Cavalry Brigade went to PLACHY BUYON.	RAB
	22nd to	31st	— Nil —	RAB
			During this month the following officers joined the Brigade. Lieut G. F. ELLIOT MC and the following officers left Capt F BARRY to 39th Division to command a battery Lieut A.H. HORNBY MC to the Xth Corps as Second in command of a battery. " D.F. AIKENHEAD to the 11th Division " " " .	RAB

RAH[illegible] Capt & Adjt
for OC. 3rd Bde RHA
31/10/17

A5834 Wt. W4973/M687 750,000 8/16 D. D. & L. Ltd. Forms/C.2118/13

2nd Dv

WD 17

Confidential

War Diary of

Headquarters
3rd Brigade RHA

from 1st to 30th November
1917

Volume ~~XL~~ XXXIX

Army Form C. 2118.

Instructions regarding War Diaries and Intelligence Summaries are contained in F. S. Regs., Part II. and the Staff Manual respectively. Title pages will be prepared in manuscript.

WAR DIARY *or* **~~INTELLIGENCE~~ ~~SUMMARY~~.** Headquarters 3rd Brigade RHA.

(*Erase heading not required.*)

Place	Date	Hour	Summary of Events and Information	Remarks and references to Appendices
	November 1917			
RUMIGNY	10th to 11th		Nil.	
	12th		Orders were received that the Brigade less Heavy Echelon of the Ammunition Column would move to join III Corps	RAB
	13th		The Brigade less Heavy Echelon of the Ammⁿ Colⁿ marched to billets as follows:–	
			Headquarters CORBIE	
			D. Batty LA NEUVILLE	
			E Battery CORBIE	
			I Batty DAOURS	RAB
	14th		Starting 4.30 P.M the Brigade marched via MEAULTE and CLERY to bivouac at the Southern end of VAUX WOOD N of MOISLAINS.	RAB
	15th		Batteries arrived at the above camp 7.30 A.M. The Brigade now came under orders of the III rd Corps.	RAB

A5834 Wt. W4973/M687 750,000 8/16 D. D. & L. Ltd. Forms/C.2118/13

Army Form C. 2118.

Instructions regarding War Diaries and Intelligence Summaries are contained in F. S. Regs., Part II. and the Staff Manual respectively. Title pages will be prepared in manuscript.

WAR DIARY
or
~~INTELLIGENCE~~ SUMMARY.
(Erase heading not required.)

Headquarters 3rd Brigade RHA

Place	Date	Hour	Summary of Events and Information	Remarks and references to Appendices
	November 1917			
VAUX WOOD	16th		Orders were received that Batteries would go into action under the 20th Divisional Artillery on the night 18/19th	RAB
	17th		Parties went forward to reconnoitre battery positions North of GOUZEAUCOURT and to lay out lines of fire	RAB
	18th		At 2 P.M. ~~at~~ D and E Batterys detachments were sent up to a position of readiness near their battery positions. After dark guns were put into action in positions ½ mile NE of GOUZEAUCOURT immediately North of the main CAMBRAI Road, wagon lines and J Batterys detachments remaining at VAUX WOOD.	RAB
	19th		Headquarters moved to the Quarry on the North Eastern outskirts of GOUZEAUCOURT. At 7.30 P.M. wagon lines moved from VAUX WOOD to an area just South of the FINS - GOUZEAUCOURT road and half way between these two villages	RAB

A5834 Wt. W4973/M687 750,000 8/16 D. D. & L. Ltd. Forms/C.2118/13

Army Form C. 2118.

Instructions regarding War Diaries and Intelligence Summaries are contained in F. S. Regs., Part II. and the Staff Manual respectively. Title pages will be prepared in manuscript.

WAR DIARY
or.
~~INTELLIGENCE SUMMARY.~~
(Erase heading not required.)

Headquarters 3rd Brigade RHA

Place	Date	Hour	Summary of Events and Information	Remarks and references to Appendices
	November 1917			
GOUZEAUCOURT	20th		Zero hour for III rd Corps attack was 6.20 Am. at which hour all guns opened fire. The barrage allotted to 3rd Brigade RHA started on the enemy defences W. of LA VACQUERIE and after 8 successive lifts spread out over a period of 3½ hours finished 500 yards in advance of the Brown Line (the Second Infantry objective) and 2000 yards South west of the Southern outskirts of MASNIERES.	
			A party of two telephone operators and 8 linesmen from the Brigade under 2Lt R. B. JOHNSON 4th Hussars (attached Bde HQ) was detailed to lay a forward line for the use of the F.O.O. sent forward by the Right Group of the 20th Div. Artillery. 2nd Lieut G P HEDGES (Ammn Colm attached E Batty) was detailed to take charge of a party of visual Signallers for the use of the same FOO, in case telephone communications failed.	

Instructions regarding War Diaries and Intelligence Summaries are contained in F. S. Regs., Part II. and the Staff Manual respectively. Title pages will be prepared in manuscript.

WAR DIARY
or
~~INTELLIGENCE SUMMARY.~~
(Erase heading not required.)

Headquarters 3rd Brigade RHA.

Army Form C. 2118.

Place	Date	Hour	Summary of Events and Information	Remarks and references to Appendices
	November 1917			
GOUZEAUCOURT	20th	(Continued)	1.30 P.M. The Canadian Cavalry Brigade were seen moving forward and teams were immediately sent for. All batteries were limbered up at 2.45 and ready to join their Cavalry Brigades as they moved up the Cavalry Tracks. The 2nd Cavalry Division moved to a position of readiness in the low ground half way between MARCOING and LA VACQUERIE arriving there about 7 P.M. Batteries were disposed as follows:-	
			D Batty with the 3rd Cavalry Brigade (the leading Brigade)	
			E Batty with the 5th Cavalry Brigade, in rear of the 3rd Cavalry Brigade.	
			J Battery at VILLERS PLUICH with the 4th Cavalry Brigade.	
			The light Echelon Subsections of the Ammunition Column under Lieut. C.H. BORTHWICK in rear of J Batty at VILLERS PLUICH.	RHB
	21st		Dispositions remained as above.	
			At 4.30 P.M. the 2nd Cavalry Division withdrew to the VILLERS FAUCON Area.	

A5834 Wt. W4973/M687 750,000 8/16 D. D. & L. Ltd. Forms/C.2118/13

Army Form C. 2118.

Instructions regarding War Diaries and Intelligence Summaries are contained in F. S. Regs., Part II. and the Staff Manual respectively. Title pages will be prepared in manuscript.

WAR DIARY
or
~~INTELLIGENCE~~ SUMMARY.
(*Erase heading not required.*)

Headquarters 3rd Brigade RHA.

Place	Date	Hour	Summary of Events and Information	Remarks and references to Appendices
	November 1917			
	21st (Continued)		The 3rd Brigade RHA returned to former wagon lines between GOUZEAUCOURT and FINS except J Batty and the Light Echelon of the Ammunition Column who remained at VILLERS PLUICH	RAB
	22nd		At 10.30 Am. the Brigade moved to join the remainder of the 2nd Cavalry Division near VILLERS FAUCON, where batteries joined their Cavalry Brigades.	
			Lieut H.V. DANGAR RHA joined the Brigade from the 30th Division	RAB
	23rd		The Division was now under orders to move at 1 hours notice.	
			At 3.50 P.M. orders were received that the Division would move at once to an area N. of FINS. Batteries remained with their Cavalry Brigades.	RAB
	24th		At 2.30 P.M. Camps were moved to an area S. of DESSART WOOD.	RAB

A5834 Wt. W4973/M687 750,000 8/16 D. D. & L. Ltd. Forms/C.2118/13

Instructions regarding War Diaries and Intelligence Summaries are contained in F. S. Regs., Part II. and the Staff Manual respectively. Title pages will be prepared in manuscript.

WAR DIARY
or
~~INTELLIGENCE SUMMARY.~~

(*Erase heading not required.*)

Headquarters 3rd Brigade RHA.

Army Form C. 2118.

Place	Date	Hour	Summary of Events and Information	Remarks and references to Appendices
	November 1917.			
DESSART WOOD	25th.		At 7 A.M. the Division moved to a position of Readiness between RIBECOURT and FLESQUIERES, with a view to following up the Infantry attack from BOURLON WOOD	RAB
			At 5 P.M. the Division moved back to the former camp near DESSART WOOD	RAB
	26th.		Orders received at 4.30 P.M. that the 3rd Brigade RHA would move ~~= ===~~ to FLESQUIERES. Batteries marched at 7.15 P.M. to a rendez-vous between FLESQUIERES and RIBECOURT arriving there at 10 P.M. The Brigade Commander reported to the CRA Guards Division under whose orders the Brigade was now placed. Batteries went into action in positions on the northern slopes of the valley 500 yards east of FLESQUIERES. Heavy rain and snow and a strong wind made conditions difficult. All guns were in action and	

Instructions regarding War Diaries and Intelligence Summaries are contained in F. S. Regs., Part II. and the Staff Manual respectively. Title pages will be prepared in manuscript.

WAR DIARY
or
INTELLIGENCE SUMMARY.
(*Erase heading not required.*)

Headquarters 3rd Brigade RHA.

Army Form C. 2118.

Place	Date	Hour	Summary of Events and Information	Remarks and references to Appendices
	November 1917			
FLESQUIERES	26th (Contd)		line of fire laid out soon after midnight. Headquarters were established in the HINDENBURG SUPPORT LINE at the South Eastern edge of FLESQUIERES. Wagon lines were situated near TRESCAULT.	RAB
	27th		At 6.20 am the Guards Division with the 62nd Division on their left attacked FONTAINE. The task allotted to the 3rd Brigade RHA was to cover LA FOLIE WOOD with the object of keeping down Machine Gun fire from there. In spite of most adverse weather conditions objectives were gained but subsequently lost in the face of heavy Counter attacks.	RAB
	28th		Dispositions remained unchanged. Barrage lines ordered for this Brigade covered a breadth of 1500 yards running in a N.N.W. direction from the S.W. corner of LA FOLIE WOOD.	RAB
	29th		Situation unchanged.	RAB

Army Form C. 2118.

Instructions regarding War Diaries and Intelligence Summaries are contained in F. S. Regs., Part II. and the Staff Manual respectively. Title pages will be prepared in manuscript.

WAR DIARY
or
~~INTELLIGENCE SUMMARY.~~ Headquarters 3rd Brigade RHA.

(Erase heading not required.)

Place	Date	Hour	Summary of Events and Information	Remarks and references to Appendices
	November 1917			
Nr FLESQUIERES.	30th		At 5.55 am batteries carried out harassing fire on their SOS lines.	
			At 9.45 am in reply to a very heavy enemy bombardment of BOURLON WOOD and our lines N.W. of it all Batteries were ordered to open on SOS lines.	
			At 12 noon owing to the serious situation on our left (about MOEUVRES) teams were brought up to a position of readiness N. of RIBECOURT.	
			At 12.45 pm an enemy concentration near LA FOLIE WOOD was reported and batteries were turned on to deal with it.	
			At 6 pm report was received that GOUZEAUCOURT, lost in the morning had been recaptured by the Guards, and that the line remained intact both on the III & VII Corps fronts.	
			Gun teams were consequently sent back to their wagon lines.	RM

R. Archer Capt.
for Lieut Col RHA
Comdg 3rd Bde RHA.

A5834 Wt. W4973/M687 750,000 8/16 D. D. & L. Ltd. Forms/C.2118/13

2nd Cav Div

Vol 18

CONFIDENTIAL

WAR DIARY

OF

Headquarters
3rd Brigade RHA

from 1st to 31st December 1917

Volume XL

Instructions regarding War Diaries and Intelligence Summaries are contained in F. S. Regs., Part II. and the Staff Manual respectively. Title pages will be prepared in manuscript.

WAR DIARY
or
~~INTELLIGENCE SUMMARY.~~
(Erase heading not required.)

Army Form C. 2118.

Headquarters 3rd Brigade RHA.

Place	Date	Hour	Summary of Events and Information	Remarks and references to Appendices
VENDELLES.	December 24th	&	26th The ~~Operation~~ patrol went out again as on the 23rd but with the same result in each case.	RHB
	25th – 29th		– Nil –	
	30th		On the regrouping of the artillery covering the Dismounted Cavalry Division front ~~the~~ A Battery RHA whose position was situated in the low ground half way between TEANCOURT and LE VERGUIER, were added to the sub group which remained the left sub-group of the right group of the Cavalry Divisional Artillery.	RHB
	31st		I and Q Batteries RHA were withdrawn to their wagon lines at BOUCLY and BERNES respectively.	RHB

31-12-17

[signature] Capt
for Lieut Col RHA
Comdg 3rd Bde RHA.

Instructions regarding War Diaries and Intelligence Summaries are contained in F. S. Regs., Part II. and the Staff Manual respectively. Title pages will be prepared in manuscript.

WAR DIARY or ~~INTELLIGENCE SUMMARY.~~ Headquarters 3rd Brigade RHA

(Erase heading not required.)

Army Form C. 2118.

Place	Date	Hour	Summary of Events and Information	Remarks and references to Appendices
Near FLESQUIERES	December 1st		From 5.30 to 6.30 Am harassing fire was carried out - all guns searching back 500 yards from their SOS lines. At about 1.30 P.m a heavy enemy bombardment opened on our lines from CONTAIGN northwards, and at 2 P.m the SOS signal was sent up from CONTAIGN to which all batteries replied. No infantry action followed however and at the end of about 40 minutes the hostile bombardment died down.	RAB
	2nd		From 5.30 to 6.30 Am harassing fire was carried out as yesterday - Otherwise a quiet day and batteries were not called upon to shoot.	RAB
	3rd		Immediately after day-break a heavy enemy barrage was put down on our positions from CONTAIGN southwards as far as GONNELIEU and an attack followed as a result of which we were reported to have lost MARCOING. For some hours the situation remained obscure and the position of our troops south of the BOIS DES NEUF was uncertain. As a precautionary measure teams were sent for and assembled in a position of readiness	

Instructions regarding War Diaries and Intelligence Summaries are contained in F. S. Regs., Part II. and the Staff Manual respectively. Title pages will be prepared in manuscript.

WAR DIARY
or
~~INTELLIGENCE SUMMARY.~~ Headquarters 3rd Brigade RHA

(Erase heading not required.)

Army Form C. 2118.

Place	Date	Hour	Summary of Events and Information	Remarks and references to Appendices
Near FLESQUIERES	December 1st		From 5.30 to 6.30 Am harassing fire was carried out - all guns searching back 500 yards from their SOS lines. At about 1.30 P.m a heavy enemy bombardment opened on our lines from CONTAIGN northwards, and at 2 P.m the S.O.S. signal was sent up from CONTAIGN to which all batteries replied. No infantry action followed however and at the end of about 40 minutes the hostile bombardment died down.	RAB
	2nd		From 5.30 to 6.30 Am harassing fire was carried out as yesterday - Otherwise a quiet day and batteries were not called upon to shoot.	RAB
	3rd		Immediately after day-break a heavy enemy barrage was put down on our positions from CONTAIGN southwards as far as GONNELIEU and an attack followed as a result of which we were reported to have lost MARCOING. For some hours the situation remained obscure and the position of our troops south of the BOIS DES NEUF was uncertain. As a precautionary measure teams were sent for and assembled in a position of readiness	

A5834 Wt. W4973/M687 750,000 8/16 D. D. & L. Ltd. Forms/C.2118/13

Instructions regarding War Diaries and Intelligence Summaries are contained in F. S. Regs., Part II. and the Staff Manual respectively. Title pages will be prepared in manuscript.

WAR DIARY or ~~INTELLIGENCE SUMMARY~~. Headquarters 3rd Brigade RHA

(Erase heading not required.)

Army Form C. 2118.

Place	Date	Hour	Summary of Events and Information	Remarks and references to Appendices
Near FLESQUIERES	December 3rd		(Continued) North of RIBECOURT. In view of the now somewhat advanced position of batteries it was thought necessary to post a protecting picquet on the ridge on the right front of the battery positions. A platoon of the South Staffordshire Regiment was detailed by the 176th Infantry Brigade to carry out this mission. At 9.30 P.M. it was reported that the situation on our right around MARCOING was well in hand and teams were consequently sent back to their wagon lines.	RAB
	4th.		A quiet day. Orders were received that the Brigade would withdraw during the night of 4th/5th to positions in the valley running from RIBECOURT to HAVRINCOURT, in accordance with infantry plans to withdraw to a line running N.W. & S.E. along the GRAINCOURT MARCOING Road. Batteries moved as follows:- D Batty at Dusk to a position on the North side of the GRAND RAVINE 1500 yards W. of RIBECOURT. E Batty at 10.30 P.M. to a position South of the GRAND RAVINE 1600 yards W. of RIBECOURT.	RAB

Instructions regarding War Diaries and Intelligence Summaries are contained in F. S. Regs., Part II. and the Staff Manual respectively. Title pages will be prepared in manuscript.

WAR DIARY Headquarters
or
~~INTELLIGENCE SUMMARY.~~ 3rd Brigade RHA.
(Erase heading not required.)

Army Form C. 2118.

Place	Date	Hour	Summary of Events and Information	Remarks and references to Appendices
Between RIBECOURT & HAVRINCOURT	December 5th		At 4 A.M. 'J' Batty moved to a position 300 yards North of the GRAND RAVINE 1500 yards West of RIBECOURT. Brigade Headquarters moved to dug-outs in the same area when all guns had been withdrawn from the forward positions. The zone covered for Barrage purposes now extended 1000 yards in a direction parallel to the GRAINCOURT – MARCOING Road at a distance of 400 yards on the North East Side of that road with its right flank on the CONTAIGN – FLESQUIERES road. During the night harassing fire was carried out for which purpose all guns searched back on barrage lines.	RAB
	6th		In the early morning barrage lines were moved to cover approaches towards FLESQUIERES up the valley running East & West 400 yards East of FLESQUIERES. They were subsequently changed to cover the approaches nearer the village. At 3.5 P.M. S.O.S. Barrage was called for and batteries ~~[illegible]~~ kept up continuous fire for 1½ hours. The cause of the alarm has not been discovered for some while but was probably due to –	

A5834 Wt. W4973/M687 750,000 8/16 D. D. & L. Ltd. Forms/C.2118/13

Army Form C. 2118.

Instructions regarding War Diaries and Intelligence Summaries are contained in F. S. Regs., Part II. and the Staff Manual respectively. Title pages will be prepared in manuscript.

WAR DIARY or ~~INTELLIGENCE SUMMARY.~~

(Erase heading not required.)

Headquarters 3rd Brigade RHA

Place	Date	Hour	Summary of Events and Information	Remarks and references to Appendices
Between RIBECOURT + HAVRINCOURT	December 6th (Cont'd)		a considerable amount of enemy movement about and to the north of ORIVAL WOOD. The Germans were probably merely following up our retirement.	RAB
	7th.		Orders were received that the Brigade would withdraw to the wagon lines to-night and march on the 8th to the Cavalry Corps area. A good deal of harassing fire was carried out during the day in the ORIVAL WOOD area. Batteries withdrew to their wagon lines at the South western edge of HAVRINCOURT WOOD after dusk.	RAB
	8th.		The Brigade marched to BOUCLY (South of TINCOURT) and was billeted there in huts. Under orders from Cavalry Corps batteries were each to put one section into action on the night of the 9th and the remainder of batteries were to go in on the night of 10th. The Brigade now came under the 5th Cavalry Division for administration and supplies.	RAB
	9th.		The OC RHA and Batty Commanders reconnoitred positions and a section of each battery went into action after dusk.	RAB

A5834 Wt. W4973/M687 750,000 8/16 D. D. & L. Ltd. Forms/C.2118/13

Instructions regarding War Diaries and Intelligence Summaries are contained in F. S. Regs., Part II. and the Staff Manual respectively. Title pages will be prepared in manuscript.

WAR DIARY
or
~~INTELLIGENCE SUMMARY.~~ Headquarters 3rd Brigade RHA.

(*Erase heading not required.*)

Army Form C. 2118.

Place	Date	Hour	Summary of Events and Information	Remarks and references to Appendices
	December			
VENDELLES.	10th		Brigade Headquarters moved to VENDELLES. Remaining sections of each battery went into action after dusk. Batteries were situated as follows:- D and E on the North Eastern edge of CAUBRIERES WOOD 1000 yards South of LE VERGUIER, J Battery in the low ground 1000 yards South East of VENDELLES. Q Battery RHA also forming part of the Group were situated 400 yards east of J Battery. The four batteries formed a sub-group of the Cavalry Division Artillery Group commanded by Lieut Colonel A.R. WAINRIGHT, which came under the 24th Divisional Artillery. The Barrage lines covered a front of 1000 yards on the western Edge of ASCENSION WOOD.	RHB
	11th to 13th		Nil	
	14th		A section of J Battery was moved forward to PARKEN COPSE (2000 yards SE. of LE VERGUIER)	RHB
	15th		During the night J. Battery's forward section in cooperation with	

Instructions regarding War Diaries and Intelligence Summaries are contained in F. S. Regs., Part II. and the Staff Manual respectively. Title pages will be prepared in manuscript.

WAR DIARY or ~~INTELLIGENCE~~ SUMMARY.

(Erase heading not required.)

Headquarters 3rd Brigade RHA

Army Form C. 2118.

Place	Date	Hour	Summary of Events and Information	Remarks and references to Appendices
VENDELLES.	December 15th	(Continued).	Groups on the right and left carried out harassing fire on roads, & tracks leading west from BELLENGLISE	RAB
			Harassing fire as above was repeated during the night	RAB
	16th		Capt C.W. ALLFREY D Batty RHA left to join the 21st Division as Battery Commander	
	17th		— Nil —	
	18th		Between 7.30 and 9 P.M. tracks and Company Headquarters west of BELLENGLISE were fired on with bursts of fire at irregular intervals by J's forward Section.	RAB
	19th to 21st		— Nil —	
	22nd		J Battery's forward Section was withdrawn to their main position South East of VENDELLES.	
	23rd		A large patrol was sent out at 4 P.m. by the Essex Yeomanry to reconnoitre ASCENSION WOOD and the two small woods east of it, and in connection with this operation D and E Batteries were ordered to stand by in order to fire on any of these woods if they were found to be occupied by the enemy. All 3 woods were found unoccupied and batteries did not fire.	RAB

A5834 Wt. W4973/M687 750,000 8/16 D. D. & L. Ltd. Forms/C.2118/13

Instructions regarding War Diaries and Intelligence Summaries are contained in F. S. Regs., Part II. and the Staff Manual respectively. Title pages will be prepared in manuscript.

WAR DIARY
or
~~INTELLIGENCE SUMMARY.~~
(Erase heading not required.)

Headquarters
3rd Brigade RHA.

Army Form C. 2118.

Place	Date	Hour	Summary of Events and Information	Remarks and references to Appendices
VENDELLES	December 24th	&	26th The ~~operation~~ patrol went out again as on the 23rd but with the same result in each case	RMB
	25th – 29th		– Nil –	
	30th		On the regrouping of the artillery covering the Dismounted Cavalry Division front, A Battery RHA whose position was situated in the low ground half way between JEANCOURT and LE VERGUIER, were added to the sub group which remained the left sub-group of the right group of the Cavalry Divisional Artillery.	RMB
	31st		I and Q Batteries RHA were withdrawn to their wagon lines at BOUCLY and BERNES respectively.	RMB

31-12-17

[illegible] Capt
for Lieut Col RHA
Comdg 3rd Bde RHA.

A5834 Wt. W4973/M687 750,000 8/16 D. D. & L. Ltd. Forms/C.2118/13

Confidential

WO 95/19

War Diary of

3rd Bde. R.H.A.

From 1st Jan. 1918 to 31. Jan. 1918

Volume 41

Instructions regarding War Diaries and Intelligence Summaries are contained in F. S. Regs., Part II. and the Staff Manual respectively. Title pages will be prepared in manuscript.

WAR DIARY
or
INTELLIGENCE SUMMARY.
(Erase heading not required.)

Army Form C. 2118.

Place	Date	Hour	Summary of Events and Information	Remarks and references to Appendices
VENDELLES	Jan 1st	to 3rd	NIL	
ditto	3rd		Lt Col A MELLOR DSO RHA took over temporary command of the Right Group Cav: Div. Artillery, & Major R C MAITLAND DSO RHA. commanded MELLORS Sub-group in his absence.	
ditto	4th	to 7th	NIL	
ditto	8th		A, the and D Bty withdrew to their wagon lines.	
ditto	9th	to 10th	NIL.	
ditto	11th		Wagon Lines of the Brigade moved from BOUCHY to CAULAINCOURT. "D" Bty marched to VILLERS-CARBONNEL where they came under orders of RHA Cavalry Corps. An RHA School was to be formed there, with Major NORTON as Commandant, and the Battery as depot Battery.	
ditto	12th	to 15th	NIL	
ditto	16th		The relief of MELLORS Sub-group by the 311th Army Bde. RFA commenced, half of A. Bty RHA & half of E Bty RHA were relieved by similar portions of A/311 & C/311 respectively, & withdrew to their wagon lines.	
ditto	17th		The remainder of A & E RHA Batteries were relieved, & withdrew to their wagon lines.	
ditto	18th		Brigade HQrs were relieved by the HQrs 311th Army Bde. RFA. under the command of Lt Col PREESTON, the Group now became PREESTONS Group.	
ditto	19th	to 31st	This period was spent by Batteries in training. On 26th "J" supplied 1 Gun to Cavalry Divisional Artillery for anti tank purposes. 2/Lt R.K.A. KENNEDY joined this Bde from 84th Army Bde R.F.A. On 28th "D" RHA supplied one gun to 24th DA for anti tank purposes.	

[illegible] Lt Col RHA
[illegible] RHA

CONFIDENTIAL

War Diary

of

Headquarters 3rd Bde RHA.

1st – 28th February 1918.

Army Form C. 2118.

Instructions regarding War Diaries and Intelligence Summaries are contained in F. S. Regs., Part II. and the Staff Manual respectively. Title pages will be prepared in manuscript.

WAR DIARY
or
~~INTELLIGENCE SUMMARY.~~
(Erase heading not required.)

Headquarters 3rd Brigade RHA

Feby 1918.

Place	Date	Hour	Summary of Events and Information	Remarks and references to Appendices
CAULAINCOURT	February 1st	- 11th	Nothing of importance to record - The Brigade (less D Batty RHA and the SAA section Ammunition Column) remained in mobile reserve to Cavalry Corps. 'D' Batty RHA continued to do duty as depot battery for the Cavalry Corps RHA School and the SAA section of the Ammunition Column remained with the 2nd Cavalry Division	RMB
	12th		E and J Batteries having gone into positions on the north side of the river North West of MAISSEMY supported a raid on the enemy trenches by the Canadian Cavalry Brigade. The area raided was situated North West of BELLENGLISE and several prisoners and machine guns were captured	RMB
	13th		E & J Batteries returned to their wagon lines	RMB
	14th	- 20th	Nil	RMB
	21st.		One section of E & J Batteries respectively went into action on the South western edge of MAISSEMY	RMB
MAISSEMY	22nd		The remainder of E & J Batteries went into action at MAISSEMY. These two Batteries formed the Right Group of the Cavalry Divisional Artillery and covered the Canadian Dismounted Brigade front between BELLENGLISE	

Instructions regarding War Diaries and Intelligence Summaries are contained in F. S. Regs., Part II. and the Staff Manual respectively. Title pages will be prepared in manuscript.

WAR DIARY
or
~~INTELLIGENCE SUMMARY.~~ Headquarters 3rd Bde RHA.

(Erase heading not required.)

Army Form C. 2118.

Place	Date	Hour	Summary of Events and Information	Remarks and references to Appendices
MAISSEMY	February 22nd		(Continued) and GRICOURT. Group Headquarters were established at the Southern end of MAISSEMY	RMB
	22nd – 24th		Spent registering	RMB
	25th		At 9.30 P.m in support of a minor enterprise on the part of Lord Strathcona's Horse batteries fired 800 rounds on the enemy front line in front of PONTREUT.	RMB
	26th – 27th		Nil	RMB
	28th	–	Owing presumably to information obtained by the intelligence branch a state of immediate readiness for enemy attack was ordered.	RMB

28/2/18

Robert Cope
for OC 3rd Bde RHA.

A5834 Wt. W4973/M687 750,000 8/16 D. D. & L. Ltd. Forms/C.2118/13

3/2 Cav Div

(6202) W 11186/M1151 350,000 12/16 McA. & W., Ltd. (Est. 731) Forms/W 3091/3. Army Form W. 3091.

Vol 21

Cover for Documents.

CONFIDENTIAL

Nature of Enclosures.

WAR DIARY

OF

3RD BRIGADE R.H.A.

MARCH 1918.

Notes, or Letters written.

Instructions regarding War Diaries and Intelligence Summaries are contained in F. S. Regs., Part II. and the Staff Manual respectively. Title pages will be prepared in manuscript.

Army Form C. 2118.

3rd Brigade RHA.

WAR DIARY
or
~~INTELLIGENCE SUMMARY~~. of MARCH. 1918.

(Erase heading not required.)

Place	Date	Hour	Summary of Events and Information	Remarks and references to Appendices
	1st to 10th		Batteries in action near MAISSEMY. except D: which was in Mobile Reserve.	[initials]
	11th		2 Sections each of E and J batteries relieved by B and C/107.	[initials]
	12th		Remaining sections came out of action.	
	13th to 19th		Brigade marched through HAM to GUIVRY and BEINES.	[initials]
	20th		At 2 pm orders received for Bde Am. Column to move to Le CAISNEL near VILLEQUIER AUMONT & to come under orders of 3rd Corps R.A.	[initials]
	21st		At 4.45 am German bombardment commenced.	[initials]
		2.30pm	E Bty went into action to cover canal bridges at JUSSY.	[initials]
		4pm	J. " " " with 190th R.F.A. Bde N E of ROUEZ covering TERGUIER.	
		"	D " " " E of the big wood South of FRIERES FAILLOUEL.	[initials]
	22nd	6am	At dawn E battery came into action near D.	
			Batteries shooting hard all day. Excellent targets during the afternoon when mist cleared & attacks from direction of TERGUIER completely held up till light failed –	[initials]

T2134. Wt. W708–776. 500000. 4/15. Sir J. C. & S.

Instructions regarding War Diaries and Intelligence Summaries are contained in F. S. Regs., Part II. and the Staff Manual respectively. Title pages will be prepared in manuscript.

WAR DIARY or INTELLIGENCE SUMMARY.

(Erase heading not required.)

Army Form C. 2118.

Place	Date	Hour	Summary of Events and Information	Remarks and references to Appendices
	22nd	8pm	E withdrew to a position S.E of VILLEQUIER AUMONT.	
		9pm	D "	
		12 midnight	J "	
			Lt Wilson of D battery wounded.	Dm
	23rd	3.30am	Orders recd to support counter attack by French at dawn.	
		6am	D & E came into action E of Z in ROUEZ. ($\frac{1}{100.000}$). J in rear of them. Fired barrage programme - Nothing was seen of the counter attack which did not appear to ever start.	
		10am	German attacks commenced on the wood E of FRIERES FAILLOUEL. The 18th Division fighting hard was pressed back by degrees and during the afternoon J. then E. & finally D batteries were withdrawn to position S.E of VILLEQUIER AUMONT.	
			Lieutenant R.C. NORTON. E battery RHA. killed.	
			At dusk our line ran through Eastern edge of VILLEQUIER AUMONT -	
			Batteries withdrew after dark to positions N of CAUMONT.	
			At night line was taken over by French troops —	Dm

T2134. Wt. W708–776. 500000. 4/15. Sir J. C. & S.

Instructions regarding War Diaries and Intelligence Summaries are contained in F. S. Regs., Part II. and the Staff Manual respectively. Title pages will be prepared in manuscript.

WAR DIARY
or
INTELLIGENCE SUMMARY.
(Erase heading not required.)

Army Form C. 2118.

Place	Date	Hour	Summary of Events and Information	Remarks and references to Appendices
	24th		Bde had orders to remain in action & support the French till 9.30am. Fired on VILLEQUIER AUMONT and RUEZ. & approaches.	
			About 9 am the line began retiring very fast and the 75 batteries retired. It was extremely difficult to make out the situation but the Germans appeared to have occupied the BOIS de CAUMONT.	
			T battery was withdrawn first then E & then D. the last battery moving about 12 noon.	
			Batteries retired through BETHANCOURT & came into action S.W. of CAILLOUEL.	
			About 4pm retired to position W of CREPIGNY.	
			Captain & adjt R.A. BECK. wounded.	RM
	25th		At 3.30 am the line was withdrawn to CREPIGNY & brigade was withdrawn to N.E of BABOEUF.	
			At 10.30 am under orders of 18th Divn R.A. Brigade moved via MERLINCOURT to a position between VARESNES and BRETIGNY & barraged approaches from GRANDRU.	
		11pm	All ammunition was expended at 4.30pm & the brigade was ordered to move to WARSY West of ROYE. These orders were cancelled & brigade ordered to CARLEPONT.	RM

T2134. Wt. W708—776. 500000. 4/15. Sir J. C. & S.

Instructions regarding War Diaries and Intelligence Summaries are contained in F. S. Regs., Part II. and the Staff Manual respectively. Title pages will be prepared in manuscript.

WAR DIARY
or
INTELLIGENCE SUMMARY.
(*Erase heading not required.*)

Army Form C. 2118.

Place	Date	Hour	Summary of Events and Information	Remarks and references to Appendices
	26th		Marched to THOUROTTE and LONGUEIL in direction of COMPIEGNE – The ammunition column rejoined the Brigade.	RM
	27th		Moved to ESTREE St DENNIS & joined 2nd Cavalry Divn.	RM
	28th	6 am	Division ordered to march at once as Germans had broken through at MONTDIDIER Batteries accompanied their Cavalry brigades.	
			On arrival at CHEPOIX it was found the gap had been filled & batteries reconnoitred positions to cover villages W of MONTDIDIER.	
			E & J batteries billetted at BACOUEL. D at WELLES PERENNES.	RM
	29th		Marched to area South of AMIENS : Dn. H.Q. at BOVES.	RM
	30th		D Battery (with 3rd Cav: Bde & Canadian Cav. Bde) assisted in attack on wood N of MOREUIL. Cavalry cleared the wood but the infantry retired after they had relieved the cavalry night of 30/31.	
			D. Battery was lent to 8th Division who took over from 3rd & Can: Cav: Bdes.	
			E & J with 4th & 5th Cavalry brigades remained in BOIS L'ABBE' E of AMIENS.	RM
	31st		D Battery moved to a position SE of HAILLES.	
			About 4 pm J battery came into action near BERTEAUCOURT.	RM

Army Form C. 2118.

WAR DIARY
or
INTELLIGENCE SUMMARY.
(*Erase heading not required.*)

Instructions regarding War Diaries and Intelligence Summaries are contained in F. S. Regs., Part II. and the Staff Manual respectively. Title pages will be prepared in manuscript.

Place	Date	Hour	Summary of Events and Information	Remarks and references to Appendices
			Batteries fired a great deal during the retreat & good targets were obtained. On an average 1500 rounds a battery was fired daily. The position of the Column (at GUIVRY) and the fact that it was under orders of the 2nd Cav. Divn while batteries were under 3rd Corps made ammunition supply difficult.	DM
			D Phillips Lt Col RHA Comd 3rd Bde RHA	

A5834 Wt. W4973/M687 750,000 8/16 D. D. & L. Ltd. Forms/C.2118/13

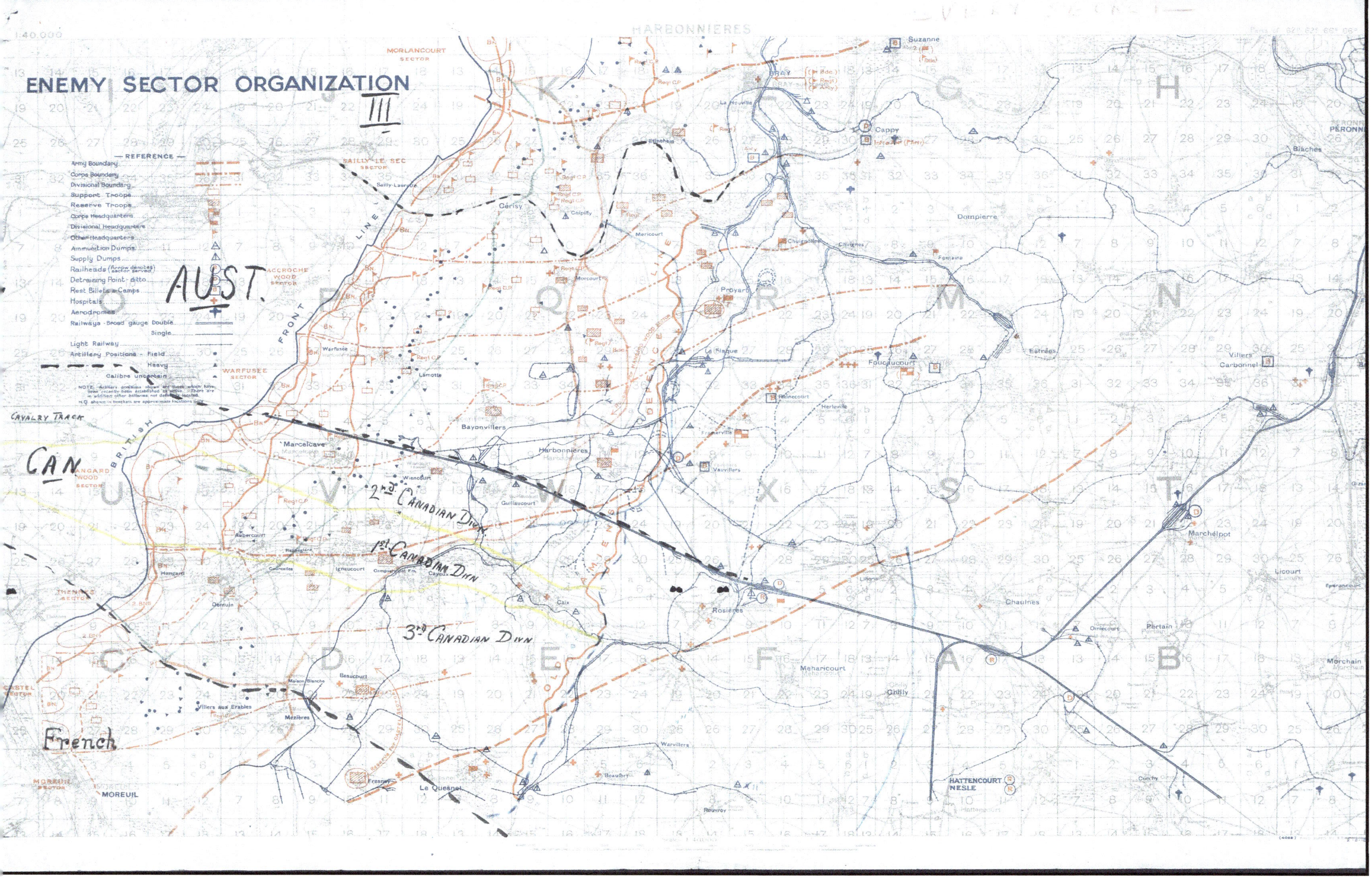
ENEMY SECTOR ORGANIZATION
III
— REFERENCE —
Army Boundary
Corps Boundary
Divisional Boundary
Support Troops
Reserve Troops
Corps Headquarters
Divisional Headquarters
Other Headquarters
Ammunition Dumps
Supply Dumps
Railheads
Detraining Point - ditto
Rest Billets & Camps
Hospitals
Aerodromes
Railways - Broad gauge Double
Single
Light Railway
Artillery Positions - Field
Heavy
Calibre uncertain
AUST.
CAN
French
CAVALRY TRACK
2nd CANADIAN DIVN
1st CANADIAN DIVN
3rd CANADIAN DIVN
BRITISH FRONT LINE
MORLANCOURT SECTOR
SAILLY-LE-SEC SECTOR
ACCROCHE WOOD SECTOR
WARFUSEE SECTOR
HARBONNIERES
Suzanne
Bray
Cappy
Dompierre
Chuignolles
Proyart
Foucaucourt
Estrées
Villers Carbonnel
Péronne
Biaches
Cerisy
Morcourt
Warfusée
Lamotte
Bayonvillers
Marcelcave
Harbonnières
Framerville
Vauvillers
Rainecourt
Herleville
Wiencourt
Guillaucourt
Caix
Rosières
Lihons
Chaulnes
Marchélpot
Licourt
Omiécourt
Pertain
Morchain
Méharicourt
Chilly
Hattencourt
Nesle
Warvillers
Beaufort
Rouvroy
Le Quesnel
Fresnoy
Beaucourt
Maison Blanche
Mézières
Villers aux Erables
Demuin
Hangard
Aubercourt
Ignaucourt
Cayeux
Moreuil
MOREUIL SECTOR
CASTEL SECTOR
THENNES SECTOR
HANGARD WOOD SECTOR

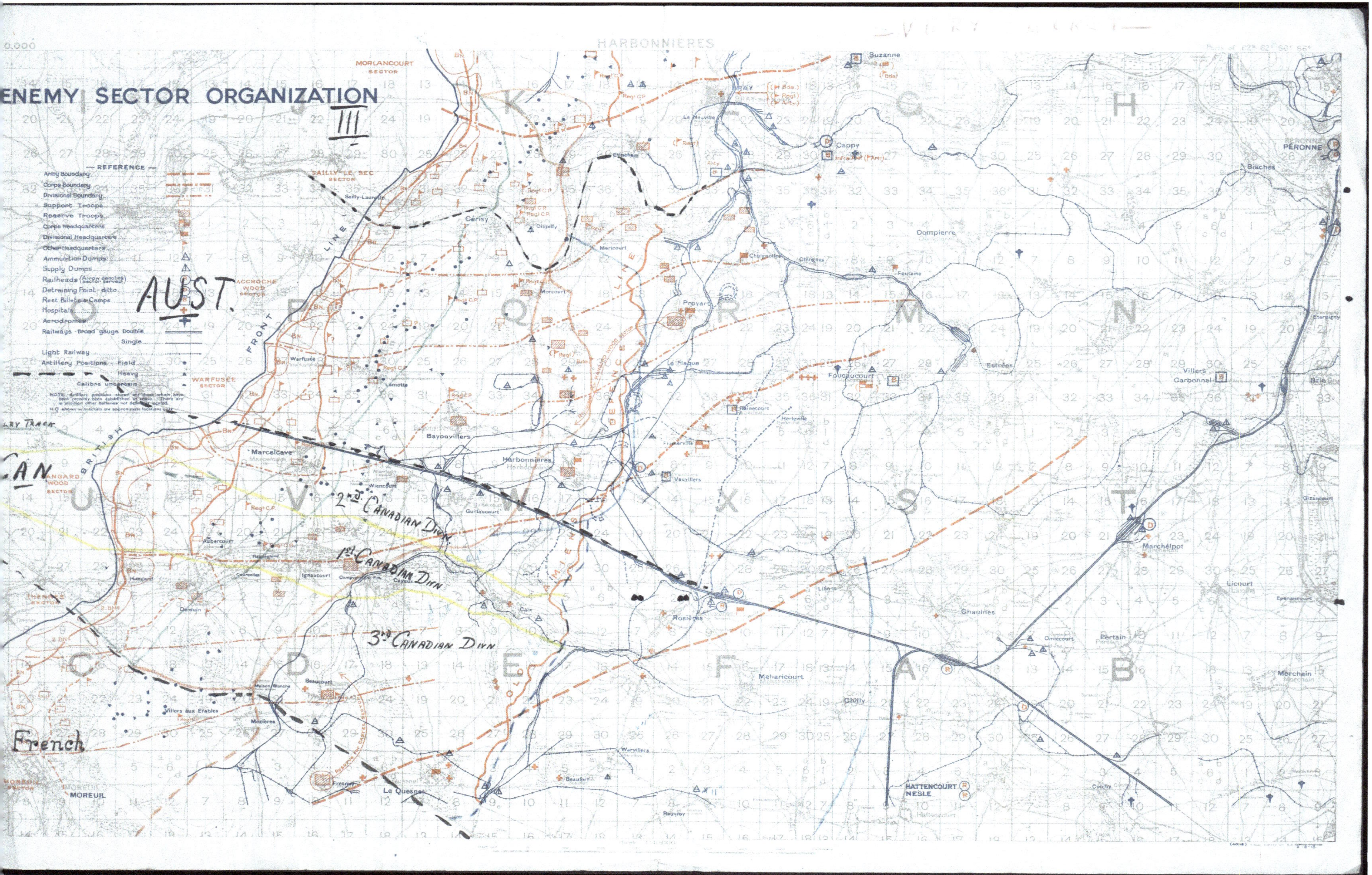

ENEMY SECTOR ORGANIZATION
III
HARBONNIERES
— REFERENCE —
Army Boundary
Corps Boundary
Divisional Boundary
Support Troops
Reserve Troops
Corps Headquarters
Divisional Headquarters
Other Headquarters
Ammunition Dumps
Supply Dumps
Railheads
Detraining Point - ditto
Rest Billets & Camps
Hospitals
Aerodromes
Railways - Broad gauge Double
Single
Light Railway
Artillery Positions - Field
Heavy
Calibre uncertain
AUST.
CAN
French
BRITISH FRONT LINE
2nd Canadian Divn
1st Canadian Divn
3rd Canadian Divn
MORLANCOURT SECTOR
SAILLY-LE-SEC SECTOR
ACCROCHE WOOD SECTOR
WARFUSEE SECTOR
HANGARD WOOD SECTOR
Suzanne
Bray
Cappy
Peronne
Biaches
Dompierre
Fontaine
Chuignolles
Chuignes
Etinehem
Cerisy
Morcourt
Mericourt
Proyart
Foucaucourt
Estrées
Villers Carbonnel
Brie
Eterpigny
Lamotte
Warfusee
Bayonvillers
Harbonnieres
Marcelcave
Wiencourt
Guillaucourt
Vauvillers
Framerville
Rainecourt
Herleville
Marchélpot
Licourt
Lihons
Chaulnes
Rosières
Caix
Aubercourt
Ignaucourt
Cayeux
Hangard
Demuin
Beaucourt
Mezieres
Villers aux Erables
Fresnoy
Le Quesnel
Beaufort
Warvillers
Rouvroy
Meharicourt
Chilly
Omiecourt
Pertain
Hattencourt
Nesle
Curchy
Morchain
Moreuil

Special
SHEET
HQ 3rd Brigade
(HM)

Instructions regarding War Diaries and Intelligence Summaries are contained in F. S. Regs., Part II. and the Staff Manual respectively. Title pages will be prepared in manuscript.

WAR DIARY
~~or~~
INTELLIGENCE SUMMARY.
(Erase heading not required.)

Army Form C. 2118.

April 1918.

Head Quarters
3rd Brigade RHA

Vol 22

Place	Date	Hour	Summary of Events and Information	Remarks and references to Appendices
GENTELLES	APRIL 1918 1st		D/RHA in action at HAILLES. E/RHA in a position 500x W of farm N of DOMART. T/RHA about ½ mile W of BERTEAUCOURT. Head Quarters near Gentelles. D spent a fairly quiet day - the they were shelled in the afternoon. E and T batteries took part in the attack made by the 2nd Cav. Div. on the wood just S of Hourges which was made with great gallantry and was entirely successful. Both batteries had excellent targets and did a lot of execution - nearly 800 rounds per gun were fired. A good day.	
Near AMIENS	2nd-5th		Batteries came out of action and rejoined their Cavalry Brigade. The whole division remained in close reserve on the outskirts of AMIENS but were not engaged again.	
AILLY-le-haut-CLOCHER	6th	6am	Marched to AILLY-le-haut-clocher. Batteries marched with their Brigades and had some long & tiring marches between the 6th and 10th.	
AUXI-LE-CHATEAU	10th	3pm	Marched to AUXI-le-CHATEAU	
BOMY	12th	1pm	Marched to BOMY.	
BLARINGHEM	13th		Marched to BLARINGHEM. T Battery with the 4th Cavalry Brigade were at 1 hours notice in a position of readiness near LA BELLE HAUTESSE.	
	14th		T Battery took up a position 1 mile E of MORBECQUE to cover the wood N of LAMOTTE-aux-BOIS but did not fire & was subsequently relieved by E Battery	

Instructions regarding War Diaries and Intelligence Summaries are contained in F. S. Regs., Part II. and the Staff Manual respectively. Title pages will be prepared in manuscript.

WAR DIARY
or
INTELLIGENCE SUMMARY.
(*Erase heading not required.*)

Army Form C. 2118.

Head Quarters 3rd Brigade R.H.A.

Place	Date	Hour	Summary of Events and Information	Remarks and references to Appendices
BLARINGHEM	APRIL 15th		D Battery relieved E Battery in the forward positions. E Battery withdrew to billets in farm S. of BLARINGHEM. T Battery in billets at SERCUS and the Columns in farm near BLARINGHEM	
"	16th–20th		2nd Cav. Div. detailed Brigades in turn to be ready to support any part of the line if required – brigades thus being at from 1 to 3 hours notice. No action resulted. The time was spent in clearing up and making good deficiencies and in routine work.	
"	17th		Fitter Pereira of T Battery R.H.A. was awarded the military medal for good work done during period 22nd March to 2nd April	
"	19th		2/Lieut Kitwood joined the Brigade from 1st Division. Major R. E. Norton M.C. R.H.A. was awarded the D.S.O. B.S.M. Macdonald of D. Battery was awarded the M.C. both awards being for good services rendered during the Fifth Army's retreat.	

A5834 Wt. W4973/M687 750,000 8/16 D. D. & L. Ltd. Forms/C.2118/13

Instructions regarding War Diaries and Intelligence Summaries are contained in F. S. Regs., Part II. and the Staff Manual respectively. Title pages will be prepared in manuscript.

April 1918

WAR DIARY
or
INTELLIGENCE SUMMARY.
(Erase heading not required.)

Head Quarters 3rd Brigade R.H.A.

Army Form C. 2118.

Place	Date	Hour	Summary of Events and Information	Remarks and references to Appendices
BLARINGHEM	APRIL 20th		HQ 3rd Bde RHA in billets at BLARINGHEM. D Battery RHA at EECKES. E/RHA at BOESINGHEM. T/RHA at SERCUS. Column near BLARINGHEM. Capt T.A.M. Bond RHA joined from 17th Brigade RHA and took over duties of adjutant	Ref map HAZEBROUCK 1:100000
"	25th		D/RHA moved to LYNDE	
"	26th		Divisional Commander inspected horses of D/RHA & Column	
"	27th		Casting parade by D.D.R. Cavalry Corps. G.O.C. RHA was present. Lieut Townsend RFA left the column on posting to Field Artillery. D/RHA moved to HEDRINGHEM	
COYECQUE	29th		Marched from BLARINGHEM to COYECQUE. Batteries marched with their Brigades. Lieut Wilkes RFA left column on posting to A.A. battery.	
"	30th		HQ and Column at COYECQUE. D/RHA at Inghem. E/RHA at MENCAS. T/RHA at WANDONNE. Capt C.F. Browne MC RHA left T Battery RHA on posting to command a Field Artillery Battery. 2/Lieut T.L.G. Tod joined from base was posted to T/RHA. 2/Lieut F.M. Boylan RFA joined from base was posted to E/RHA	

T.A.M. Bond Capt RHA
for OC 3rd Brigade RHA

A5834 Wt. W4973/M687 750,000 8/16 D. D. & L. Ltd. Forms/C.2118/13

7

CONFIDENTIAL.

Vol 23

WAR DIARY

OF

H.Q. 3rd BRIGADE R.H.A.

MAY 1918.

VOL. XLV

Hd Qrs 70. 31.5.18.

Army Form C. 2118.

Instructions regarding War Diaries and Intelligence Summaries are contained in F. S. Regs., Part II. and the Staff Manual respectively. Title pages will be prepared in manuscript.

WAR DIARY
or
INTELLIGENCE SUMMARY.

(Erase heading not required.)

Head Quarters 3rd Brigade R.H.A.

Place	Date	Hour	Summary of Events and Information	Remarks and references to Appendices
COYECQUES	1st May 1918		In billets at COYECQUES. D/R.H.A at INGHEM. E/R.H.A at MENCAS. T/R.H.A at WANDONNE. Column at COYECQUES. Routine & training	HAZEBROUCK Sheet 1:100,000
	2nd May.		Lt. Col. A. Mellor D.S.O. R.H.A. awarded a bar to the D.S.O. for distinguished services rendered during the Battle of AMIENS.	
Nr MONTCAVREL	5th		Marched to MONTESCHORE CHATEAU near MONTCAVREL. Good billets alike for men & horses. D/R.H.A at BREXENT. E/R.H.A at MARANT. T/R.H.A at INEXEN. Column at ESTREE. Division in G.H.Q. Reserve.	CALAIS 1:100,000
"	8th		Lt. ELLIS R.F.A. joined the Brigade on posting from Field Artillery & was attached to the Column. Time spent in routine & training.	
"	10th		Presentation of medal ribbons to 2nd Cavalry Div. by the Corps Commander.	
"	11th		General Seligman visited 3rd Brigade H.Q.	

A5834 Wt. W4973/M687 750,000 8/16 D. D. & L. Ltd. Forms/C.2118/13

Instructions regarding War Diaries and Intelligence Summaries are contained in F. S. Regs., Part II. and the Staff Manual respectively. Title pages will be prepared in manuscript.

WAR DIARY
or
INTELLIGENCE SUMMARY.
(Erase heading not required.)

Army Form C. 2118.

Place	Date	Hour	Summary of Events and Information	Remarks and references to Appendices
Nt MONTCAYREL	4th		Lieut T CORRIE RHA T/RHA left the Brigade on posting as 2nd in command of a Field Battery.	CALAIS Sheet 1/100,000
			Lieut A TURNER RHA appointed Captain of T/Battery	
	21st		Lieut Kennedy MC RHA left the Brigade on posting to Field Artillery.	
	21st		2/Lieut Cook RFA joined the Brigade & was posted to the Column	
	26th		2/Lieut GWC Montgomery RFA joined the Brigade & was attached temporarily to HQ	
	25th		Lieut Ellis RFA posted to T Battery RHA from the Column	
			Nothing of importance occurred during May. The time was usefully spent in routine training and conditioning the horses	
			F.A.G. [illegible] Capt. RHA for Lt Col comdg 3rd Brigade RHA	

A5834 Wt. W4973/M687 750,000 8/16 D. D. & L. Ltd. Forms/C.2118/13

(6339) Wt. W160/M3016 1,500,000 10/17 McA & W Ltd (E 1898) Forms W3091.

Army Form W.3091.

WO 95/1124

Cover for Documents.

Nature of Enclosures.

WAR DIARY

H.Q. 3RD BRIGADE R.H.A.

From 1st to 30th June, 1918.

VOL XLVI

Notes, or Letters written.

Army Form C. 2118.

Instructions regarding War Diaries and Intelligence Summaries are contained in F. S. Regs., Part II. and the Staff Manual respectively. Title pages will be prepared in manuscript.

WAR DIARY
or
INTELLIGENCE SUMMARY.
(Erase heading not required.)

Head Quarters 3rd Brigade RHA
June 1918

Place	Date	Hour	Summary of Events and Information	Remarks and references to Appendices
June	1st		In billets Head Quarters at MONTESCHORE CH near MONTCAVREL D at BREXENT E at MARANT T at INEXEN	Ref maps CALAIS ABBEVILLE 1:100,000
	3rd		Cavalry Corps Commander, with G.O.C. RHA & Divisional Commander inspected horses of 3rd Brigade RHA	
	3-30th		Routine & training Horses all doing well	
	30th		Orders suddenly received to join 3rd Army, under V Corps D & T Batteries marched to BEAURAINVILLE Remainder of Brigade marches tomorrow	

T. Cmj' Burns Capt RHA
for Lt Col cmdg 3rd Brigade RHA

(6339) Wt. W160/M3016 1,500,000 10/17 McA & W Ltd (E 1898) Forms W3091.

Army Form W.3091.

WO 95/

Cover for Documents.

Nature of Enclosures.

Confidential.

War Diary

of

Headquarters,

3rd Brigade R.H.A.

Volume 47. July 1918

Notes, or Letters written.

HEADQUARTERS,
3RD BRIGADE,
R.H.A.
No.........................
Date.......................

July 1918

Instructions regarding War Diaries and Intelligence Summaries are contained in F. S. Regs., Part II. and the Staff Manual respectively. Title pages will be prepared in manuscript.

WAR DIARY or INTELLIGENCE SUMMARY.

(Erase heading not required.)

Army Form C. 2118.

[illegible] 3rd Brigade R.H.A.

Place	Date	Hour	Summary of Events and Information	Remarks and references to Appendices
MARCHAREL area	July 1st		D & T Batteries had moved on 30th June to the BEAUMONVILLE area. The whole Brigade marched on 1st [illegible] to the BUBERS-sur-CANCHE area on the way to [illegible] V Corps [illegible] attached. A number of officers & men were [illegible] with P.U.O.	Ref maps [illegible] LENS 1/100,000
BUBERS-sur-CANCHE	2nd		Marched to CANAPLES area where night was spent.	Marching [illegible]
CANAPLES	3rd		Marched to VARENNES. [illegible] grouped with the 7th Brigade R.H.A. (Lt Col W. Clarke CMG DSO RHA) & attached to the 17th Division in close reserve.	
VARENNES	6th		Brigade moved in to bivouacs in RAINCHEVAL wood, coming under the 21st Division (in reserve) which was without its own Artillery.	
RAINCHEVAL	7th 8th		Reconnaissance of the ground over which the Brigade	

A5834 Wt. W4973/M687 750,000 8/16 D. D. & L. Ltd. Forms/C.2118/13

Instructions regarding War Diaries and Intelligence Summaries are contained in F. S. Regs., Part II. and the Staff Manual respectively. Title pages will be prepared in manuscript.

July 1918

WAR DIARY or INTELLIGENCE SUMMARY.

(Erase heading not required.)

Army Form C. 2118.

Place	Date	Hour	Summary of Events and Information	Remarks and references to Appendices
			would fight in the event of a hostile attack were carried out	[illegible]
RAINCHEVAL			F.O.O. was [illegible] & batteries [illegible] in [illegible]	LENS
	9th		Major General T. Lecky C.B. C.M.G. G.O.C. R.A. 3rd Army inspected	1:100,000
			the horses of the Brigade & expressed himself very well	
			pleased	
	10th-20th		In bivouac. Very wet weather. Bad standings for horses	
			& batteries [illegible] owing to F.O.O. [illegible]	
			reconnaissances completed	
	21st		Marched to LE CHOREY area to [illegible] 2nd Cavalry	
			Division (march order attached) [illegible]	
			their Cavalry Brigades	
	22nd		Marched to WAIL area	
	23rd		Marched to MONTCAVREL area. March table attached	
			With the exception of [illegible] being well [illegible] march	
			nothing was accomplished during [illegible] 140 miles of Northern France	
			[illegible] the [illegible] that it started from the [illegible] 30th June 1918.	

A5834 Wt. W4973/M687 750,000 8/16 D. D. & L. Ltd. Forms/C.2118/13

Instructions regarding War Diaries and Intelligence Summaries are contained in F. S. Regs., Part II. and the Staff Manual respectively. Title pages will be prepared in manuscript.

WAR DIARY
or
INTELLIGENCE SUMMARY.
(Erase heading not required.)

Army Form C. 2118.

HQ 2nd Brigade RHA
July 1918

Place	Date	Hour	Summary of Events and Information	Remarks and references to Appendices
Montcavrel area.	24th – 31st		In billets in MONTCAVREL area. Training & cleaning.	CRAY ABBEVILLE 1:100,000
			Tom [illegible] Capt. RHA [illegible] 2nd Brigade RHA	

A5834 Wt. W4973/M687 750,000 8/16 D. D. & L. Ltd. Forms/C.2118/13

Operations File

To. O.C. "D" Battery R.H.A.
O.C. "E" Battery R.H.A.
O.C. "J" Battery R.H.A.

1. The 3rd Brigade R.H.A. will march to rejoin 2nd Cavalry Division in the LE-CAUROY are tomorrow 20th inst in accordance with the attached march table.

2. All TENTS, TRENCH COVERS and other stores obtained in present area will be dumped in the quarry by the side of the road just opposite the Headquarters lines between 5.30 a.m. and 6. a.m. on the 20th inst. Receipts will be obtained from the Adjutant. Units will render lists with these stores shewing from whom they were drawn.

3. Water Troughs belonging to the Brigade should be collected to-night.

4. Medical Officer is arranging for an ambulance to convey the men with P.U.O. unable to march. Further details will be issued later.

5. Mail for the Brigade will either go direct to 2nd Cavalry Division or be collected by Headquarters, 3rd Brigade R.H.A. Rations will be delivered at destination.

6. Billeting parties should report well ahead of Units to A.A. & Q.M.G. 2nd Cavalry Division at CHATEAU LE CAUROY to obtain allocation of Billets.
"D" Battery R.H.A. will probably remain in the vicinity of LE CAUROY to-morrow night, rejoining the 3rd Cavalry Brigade next day. Further details regarding this will be issued later.

7. Supply Lorries and Amm. Sections 2nd Cavalry Division M.T.Coy. will move independantly.

8. A C K N O W L E D G E.

T.a.m. Bond
Capt, R.H.A.
19/7/18. Adjutant, 3rd Brigade R.H.A.

Copies to:-
1. 7th Brigade R.H.A.
2. 2nd Cavalry Division.
3. Amm. Sec. 2nd Cav. Div. M.T. Coy.

Ref Map. LENS. 1/100.000. MARCH TABLE FOR 20th JULY 1918.

UNIT.	STARTING POINT.	TIME.	ROUTE.	REMARKS and DESTINATION.
"E" Battery R.H.A.	Cross Roads 200 Yds. N. of the last "E" In BEAUQUESNE.	6. 0.a.m.	MARIEUX-THIEVRES HALLOY-LUCHEUX thence no restrictions.	Last Unit to be clear of THIEVRES by 8 a.m. LE-CAUROY AREA. Billets will be obtained from A.A.& Q.M.G.2nd Cav.Div.
"J" Battery R.H.A.	do.	6.15.a.m.	do.	do.
"D" Battery R.H.A.	do.	[illegible] a.m. (corrected in hand: 6.30)	do.	do.
Headquarters.3rd Brigade R.H.A.	do.	6.45.a.m.	do.	do.

D - Rebreuviette
E = Beaufort
J = Houvin

Lorry for J. at 6.30 a.m.

[illegible]
Capt. R.H.A.

CONFIDENTIAL

WAR DIARY

OF

HEADQUARTERS

3rd BRIGADE. R.H.A.

From August 1st To August 31st 1918

VOLUME No 48.

(6339) Wt. W160/M3016 1,500,000 10/17 McA & W Ltd (E 1898) Forms W3091.

Army Form W.3091.

Cover for Documents.

Nature of Enclosures.

Notes, or Letters written.

August 1918

Instructions regarding War Diaries and Intelligence Summaries are contained in F. S. Regs., Part II. and the Staff Manual respectively. Title pages will be prepared in manuscript.

WAR DIARY
or
INTELLIGENCE SUMMARY.
(Erase heading not required.)

Head Quarters 3rd Brigade R.H.A

Army Form C. 2118.

Place	Date	Hour	Summary of Events and Information	Remarks and references to Appendices
MONTCAVREL AREA	August 1st		In billets MONTCAVREL AREA Routine & training	CALAIS ABBEVILLE LENS AMIENS Sheets 1:100000
	4/5th		Orders received to march with Division at night to TOUTEFONTAINE area. March table attached. Batteries with their Cavalry Brigades.	
	5th/6th		Marched to CAOURS march table attached	
	6/7th		Marched to BREILLY march orders attached	
	7/8th		Marched to Concentration area at LONGUEAU arriving about 4.30 a.m on 8th The Division is to take part in the 4th Army operations in front of AMIENS. The Cavalry Corps for these operations is working with CANADIAN CORPS. The 1st & 3rd Cavalry Divisions attacking first. The 2nd Cavalry Division being in reserve. Operation orders & special map explaining the plan of battle & objectives attached. Zero hour was 4.20 a.m At about 6.30 a.m the 2nd Cavalry Division moved forward to	

Instructions regarding War Diaries and Intelligence Summaries are contained in F. S. Regs., Part II. and the Staff Manual respectively. Title pages will be prepared in manuscript.

WAR DIARY
or
INTELLIGENCE SUMMARY.
(Erase heading not required.)

Army Form C. 2118.

Place	Date	Hour	Summary of Events and Information	Remarks and references to Appendices
			the concentration area vacated by the other 2 Cavalry Divisions at St NICHOLAS	
			The Division then followed up the advance along a line roughly FENTELLES S. of CACHY S of VILLERS BRETONNEUX S of MARCELCAVE WIENCOURT CAIX D & T Batteries came in to action near CAIX shooting on ROSIERE en SANTERRE Divisional H.Q. remained near CAIX for the night	
NR CAIX.	9th		H Qrs wagon lines were shelled during the morning. [illegible] LINENTHAL was wounded 9 horses wounded and missing advanced at 4 p.m. in the direction of VRELY	
	10th		advanced to ROUVROY and WARVILLERS A section of D Battery with the Brigade assisted in the attack on ROUVROY was came in to action advance held up on line E of LIHONS - MEHARICOURT A great deal of bombing by enemy aeroplanes at night Moved back at night to Railway E of CAIX	

Army Form C. 2118.

WAR DIARY
or
INTELLIGENCE SUMMARY.
(Erase heading not required.)

Instructions regarding War Diaries and Intelligence Summaries are contained in F. S. Regs., Part II. and the Staff Manual respectively. Title pages will be prepared in manuscript.

Place	Date	Hour	Summary of Events and Information	Remarks and references to Appendices
	11th & 12th		spent between CAIX & VRELY. No opportunities developed for further Cavalry action	
	13th & 14th	—	moved back to just N of AUBERCOURT close to Cabanne	
	15th		Marched to BELLOY-sur-SOMME	
			The operations of the past week had been an unqualified success resulting in an advance of from 10 – 15 miles a large haul of prisoners & guns & the removal of the pressure on AMIENS	
			The 2nd Cavalry Division had not much chance of distinction as it was in reserve during the first day but the Cavalry as a whole were an undeniable success. They enabled the advance to be extremely rapid by keeping the enemy on the move during the first 2 days & the moral effect of cavalry in action was undoubtedly great. Altogether the operations augured well for the future of the Mounted Branch	

Instructions regarding War Diaries and Intelligence Summaries are contained in F. S. Regs., Part II. and the Staff Manual respectively. Title pages will be prepared in manuscript.

Army Form C. 2118.

WAR DIARY
or
INTELLIGENCE SUMMARY.
(*Erase heading not required.*)

Place	Date	Hour	Summary of Events and Information	Remarks and references to Appendices
			our casualties were light	
			D Battery had Lt Tiffeys RHA wounded Lt Robinson wounded	
			but remaining at duty 1 5 O R wounded	
			T Battery 2 O R wounded 1 O R missing	
			Column 1 O R wounded	
			Head Quarters 1 O R wounded	
			While the Brigade lost some 45 horses killed wounded	
			a large number of these casualties were caused by	
			aeroplane bombs. The horses all stuck the hard work,	
			lack of water well, came out in good condition	
	16th/17		Marched at night from BELLOY-sur-SOMME to CANAPLES	
	17/18		Marched at night to CAUMONT	
	18/19		Marched at night to LUCHEUX	
	19th		Marched at 8 pm to SAULTY	
	20th		Marched to BASSEUX The Brigade went in to action	

Instructions regarding War Diaries and Intelligence Summaries are contained in F. S. Regs., Part II. and the Staff Manual respectively. Title pages will be prepared in manuscript.

WAR DIARY
or
INTELLIGENCE SUMMARY.
(Erase heading not required.)

Army Form C. 2118.

Place	Date	Hour	Summary of Events and Information	Remarks and references to Appendices
			the same evening covering the Guards Division.	
	21st		The Brigade took part in the Barrage for the attack which commenced at 4.55 a.m. covering the Guards Division & shooting first to the N of COURCELLES	
			at 10 a.m. the Brigade advanced & came in to action again D Battery N.W. of COURCELLES E & J just S.W. of COURCELLES	
			There were no casualties fortunately	
	21/22		Brigade came out of action & marched to MONCHY-au-BOIS	
	22/23		Marched to GAUDIEMPRÉ rejoining 2nd Cavalry Division E/RHA at BASSEUX D W of MONCHY-au-BOIS J. HQrs and Column at GAUDIEMPRE	
	23rd		Major Walwyn DSO MC RHA left E Battery to take command of the Riding Troop at Woolwich Major Watson MC RHA was appointed to command E Battery	
			HQrs moved W of DOUCHY and Column to POMMIERS Batteries with their Cavalry Brigade	
	25th		The whole Brigade moved to GAUDIEMPRE & remained there till the end of the month to end a strenuous month	
			T. a. m. Bond Capt RHA	

A5834 Wt. W4973/M687 750,000 8/16 D. D. & L. Ltd. Forms/C.2118/13

War Diary

SECRET.

2nd CAVALRY DIVISION ORDER No.55.

Copy No. 4

Ref.Maps 1/100,000 CALAIS & ABBEVILLE.

4th August, 1918.

1. The Division will move to-night i/a March Table overleaf.

2. Batteries, C.F.A's and M.V.S's will march with their affiliated Brigades.

3. Distances of 200 yards will be maintained between regiments and similar units.

4. (a) No troops are to be on the march except between 9 p.m. and 3-45 a.m.

   (b) All troops and transport will be clear of roads and under cover by 4 a.m.

5. As secrecy is essential after arrival in the new area -

   (a) Watering will be carried out by small bodies at a time by routes which have been previously reconnoitred.

   (b) An officer will be detailed in each squadron and similar unit to see that personnel, horses and vehicles remain under cover during daylight, except for watering.

6. H.T.Units will move i/a instructions of A.A. & Q.M.G.

7. The undermentioned units will be collected in the present Divisional area, to be under the orders of Major S.J.HARDY, D.S.O. Scots Greys: orders as to their subsequent disposal will be issued later.

   Echelons 'B', Surplus Officers, Dismounted Men, Heavy Section Reserve Park.

8. 2nd Field Squadron will rejoin the Division i/a instructions to be issued later.

9. At 9 p.m. Divisional Hd.Qrs. will close at MONTCAVREL and open at ~~LIGESCOURT~~. TOUTE FONTAINE

ACKNOWLEDGE.

Malise Graham

Lieut.Colonel,
General Staff, 2nd Cavalry Division.

Issued at 10-40 a.m.

Normal distribution.

March Table for 4th/5th August 1918 issued with 2nd Cavalry Division Order No.55.

Unit.	Starting point.	Time.	Route.	Billeting area.	Remarks.
5th Cavalry Bde.	ø	ø	ST.REMY AUX BOIS - RAPECHY	LABROYE - FONTAINE sur MAYE.	To be clear of HESDIN - MONTREUIL road by 10.45 p.m.
4th Cavalry Bde.	BEAUCAMP X roads	ø	NAMPONT - VRON.	MACHIEL.	To be clear of S.P. by 12 midnight.
2nd Signal Sqdn. Div.H.Q.Details. H.Q.3rd Bde.R.H.A. H.Q. A.S.C. (including H.Q. A.H.T.Co.). Ammunition Column. Reserve Park Light Sec.	NEUVILLE SOUS MONTREUIL Church	10 p.m.	MONTREUIL Stn - BRIMEUX - ST REMY AUX BOIS.	LIGESCOURT-TORTEFONTAINE.	
3rd Cavalry Bde.	SORRUS.	11 p.m.	WAILLY	MAINTENAY.	4th Hussars to clear road for Reserve Park from BEUSSENT.

ø Under Brigade arrangements.

War Diary

SECRET.

2nd CAVALRY DIVISION ORDER No.56.

Copy No. 4

Ref.Maps 1/100,000 - ABBEVILLE & LENS.

5th August, 1918.

1. The Division will move to-night i/a March Table overleaf.

2. Paras. 2, 3, 4, 5 and 6 of 2nd Cav.Div.Order No.55 will hold good for to-night's march and for to-morrow.

3. 2nd Field Squadron will rejoin the Division to-night i/a March Table overleaf, less 'B' Echelon which will be sent to join Divisional 'B' Echelon at LINGRES.

4. No billeting party larger than 1 Officer and 2 O.R. per squadron will be sent on in advance before 9 p.m.

5. The Divisional Report Centre will remain at TORTEFONTAINE till further notice.

ACKNOWLEDGE.

Malise Graham

Lieut.Colonel,
General Staff, 2nd Cavalry Division.

Issued at 12-15 p.m.

Normal distribution.
19. O.C., 'B' Echelon.

March Table for 5/6th August - Issued with 2nd Cav.Div.Order No.56.

Unit.	Starting Point.	Time.	Route.	Billeting area.	Remarks.
5th Cavalry Bde.	*	*	YVRENCHEUX.	COULONVILLERS.	
2nd Field Sqdn.	*	*	HIERMONT - D in DOMLÉGER.	HANCHY - OUMONT Fm.	
4th Cavalry Bde.	*	*	(a) CRÉCY - DOMVAST. (b) FOREST-MONTIERS - NEUILLY L'HOPITAL	ST.RIQUIER.	Troops on route (a) to be clear of CRECY by 11-15 p.m. Troops on route (b) - (i) to be clear of VRON by 10 p.m. (ii) not to block Divnl. Troops on ARGENVILLERS CAOURS road.
H.Q.3rd Bde.R.H.A. Ammunition Column. Res.Pk.(Light Sec.) H.Q.,A.S.C.(incl. H.Q.,A.H.T.Coy.) Divl.Hd.Qrs.(less 'G' & 'Q' Staffs) Signal Squadron.	Road junction N.E.entrance to CRECY.	11-15 p.m.	DOMVAST - MILLENCOURT.	CAOURS.	
3rd Cavalry Bde.	*	*	VRON - NOUVION.	HAUTVILLERS.	

* Under arrangements of units concerned.

War Diary

SECRET.

2nd Cavalry Division Order No. 57.

Copy No 4

Ref.Maps 1/100,000
ABBEVILLE,LENS & AMIENS.

6th August, 1918.

1. The Division will march to-night i/a march table overleaf.

2. Paras. 2,3,4,5,6 of 2nd Cavalry Division order No. 55 will hold good except as shown on march table.

3. No billeting party larger than 1 Officer and 2 O.R. per Squadron will be sent in advance before time of march of units.

4. At 8.30.a.m. 7th instant, Divisional Headquarters will close at TORTEFONTAINE and will open at BREILLY.

ACKNOWLEDGE.

H.W. Hallcaptfor Lieut. Colonel.
General Staff, 2nd Cavalry Divn.

Issued at 12.30.a.m.

Normal distribution.

March Table for night 6th/7th August issued with 2nd Cavalry Division Order No.57.

Unit.	Starting Point.	Time.	Route.	Billeting area.	Remarks.
3rd Cavalry Bde.	Road junction 200 yards N of A in ABBEVILLE.	8.30 pm.	HALTE (S.E. of ABBEVILLE) - LONG - LE CATELET - HANGEST.	PICQUIGNY.	(a) Not to pass HANGEST before 1.am. (b) Not to block 5th Cav.Bde. or Div.Troops in PICQUIGNY.
5th Cavalry Bde.	AILLY-LE-HAUT-CLOCHER.	9.30.pm.	LA FOLIE - FLIXECOURT - LA CHAUSSEE - PICQUIGNY.	AILLY-SUR-SOMME.	Not to cross R. SOMME before midnight.
2nd Field Squad. R.E.	-do-	10.20.pm.	-do-	BREILLY.	
Div. H.Q. Signal Squad. H.Q. A.S.C. H.Q. R.H.A. Ammn.Column. Reserve Park. A.H.T. Coy.	Main road junction in VAUCHELLES.	8.30.pm.	-do-	-do-	
4th Cavalry Bde.	AILLY-LE-HAUT-CLOCHER.	11.30.pm.	LA FOLIE - FLIXECOURT.	LA CHAUSSEE.	

S E C R E T .

3rd Cavalry Brigade.
4th Cavalry Brigade.
5th Cavalry Brigade.
X C.H.H.A.
2nd Signal Squadron, R.E.

The following amendments are to be made to this office G/161/1 dated 6th August, 1918 :-

1. Para 7 (b) (i) - Line 2.

For "Brigades" read "Battalions."

2. Page 4 - para. 10 (c).

Delete "The V Call" and substitute "The Code on Popham panel".

2nd CAVALRY DIVISION
G/161/1/1.
8/8/18.
HEADQUARTERS, GENERAL STAFF

[signature]

Lieut.Colonel,
General Staff, 2nd Cavalry Division.

H.Q. 3rd Brigade R.H.A.

SECRET.

2nd Cav.Div.
G/161/1.

Copy No. 4

CONTENTS.

SECRET.

2nd Cav.Div.
G/161/1.

1. The Fourth Army are to attack the enemy's positions between the AMIENS - ROYE road (inclusive) and MORLANCOURT on a date to be notified later.

The 1st French Army are to co-operate by attacking the enemy's positions between the AVRE Valley and the AMIENS - ROYE road (exclusive).

2. The objectives and boundaries between Corps, and Divisions in the case of the Canadian Corps, and between the Fourth Army and the 1st French Army, are shown on the attached Map (issued to Brigadiers and C.R.H.A.only).

3. The troops which are to carry out this attack are as follows :-

III Corps with 10th Tank Battalion attached.
Australian Corps with 5th Tank Brigade attached.
Canadian Corps with 4th Tank Brigade attached.
Cavalry Corps with 3rd Tank Brigade attached.

The 9th Tank Battalion is to be in Army Reserve.

4. At the outset of the operations, the 3rd Cavalry Division is to work under the Canadian Corps. It is to revert to the command of the Cavalry Corps as soon as the whole of the RED Line on the Canadian Corps front has been reached by the Infantry.

5. The 3rd Tank Brigade is commanded by Brig.Genl.J.Hardress Lloyd, D.S.O., and consists of 2 Battalions of Whippet tanks :-

3rd Bn. by Lt.Col.Charrington, D.S.O., 15th Hussars.
6th Bn. by Lt.Col.C.M.Trueman, 12th Lancers.

The 6th Battalion will be attached to the 1st Cav.Divn.
The 3rd Battalion will be attached to the 3rd Cav.Divn.

6. The Cavalry track as far as the present front line is also shown on the attached map.

The track is to be marked by large white flags under arrangements to be made by 3rd Cavalry Division.

7. The Cavalry Corps is to work in the area of the Canadian Corps. Their general plan of attack is as follows with reference to the map issued as per para.2:-

(a) (i). The task of the 1st, 2nd and 3rd Canadian Divisions on the first day is to capture and hold the RED Line, except on the left of the 2nd Division front, where the task includes the capture and holding of the BLUE Line.

(ii). Should the 1st and 2nd Divisions have sufficient troops available on the first day after completing their tasks, they are to relieve the Cavalry in, or assist the Cavalry in capturing, the portions of the BLUE DOTTED Line within their own boundaries. Otherwise this task is to be carried out on the second day.

(b) (i). The task of the 3rd and 1st Cavalry Divisions with Whippet tanks of the 3rd and 6th Tank Brigades & Battalions, is to follow up the advance of the 1st and 2nd Canadian Divisions to the RED Line, where the Cavalry is to pass through the Infantry and proceed to capture and hold the BLUE DOTTED

Line.......

Line, northwards from the ROYE Road to Railway, at the same time exploiting their success east of the BLUE DOTTED Line and south and south east of the ROYE Road.

(ii). The advance of the 3rd and 1st Cavalry Divisions is to be timed so that the moment at which the Infantry leave the GREEN Line, i.e. Zero plus 4 hours, the head of the leading Brigades will have crossed our present front line, with patrols in touch with the leading Infantry.

(c) The task of the 4th Canadian Division is to advance at Zero following the 1st and 3rd Canadian Divisions, pass through them on the RED Line, and relieve the Cavalry in, or assist them in capturing, the BLUE DOTTED Line between the ROYE Road, inclusive, and the southern boundary of the 1st Canadian Division.

(d) The task of the Independent Force, which is to be composed as follows :-

Commander. Brig.Genl.R.Brutinel, C.M.G.,D.S.O., Commanding Canadian M.G.Corps.

Troops. 1st Cdn.Motor M.G.Bde.(5 batteries of 8 guns each).
2nd Cdn.Motor M.G.Bde.(5 batteries of 8 guns each).
Canadian Cyclist Bn.
1 Section 6" Newton Mortars - to be provided by G.O.C. R.A. and carried in lorries provided by G.O.C. C.M.G.C.

is to pass through the 3rd Canadian Division and make good the line of the ROYE Road between the RED Line and the BLUE DOTTED Line, forming a flank to the 3rd Cavalry Division towards the south.
As the fight progresses, the Independent Force is to continue to exploit the success down the ROYE Road, acting as a link between the most advanced cavalry and the leading Infantry.

8. The mission allotted to the Cavalry Corps is to seize and hold the outer line of the outer AMIENS Defences from the AMIENS - ROYE Road to the VILLERS BRETONNEUX - CHAULNES Railway inclusive (BLUE DOTTED Line on attached Map), and so enable the Infantry, particularly that of the Canadian Corps, to reach that line.

9. In order to carry out this mission, the 3rd Cavalry Division is to seize and hold the line from the AMIENS - ROYE Road as far as the grid line through E.16.d.0.0. (inclusive). The 1st Cavalry Division is to seize and hold the continuation of this line northwards to the VILLERS BRETONNEUX - CHAULNES Railway inclusive. This line is to be held by Cavalry until relieved by the Canadian Corps.
The 2nd Cavalry Division is to be in Reserve.

10. The areas east of AMIENS which will be occupied by the Cavalry Corps will be known as the forward concentration area.

11....

11. The movement from the forward concentration areas along the Cavalry track will take place in the following order :-

Leading Brigade 3rd Cavalry Division.
" " 1st " "
Remainder of 3rd Cavalry Division.
" " 1st " "
Whole of 2nd Cavalry Division.

The 2nd Cavalry Division will push forward reconnaissances in touch with the 1st and 3rd Cavalry Divisions, so as to be ready to support either Division.

12. The Battalions of Whippet tanks allotted to Divisions are to move simultaneously along the track, under arrangements to be made by Divisions with Commanders of Tank Battalions.

13. No dividing line can be laid down between Divisions for their advance, but the 1st Cavalry Division is instructed to hug the railway with its left, so as to give the 3rd Cavalry Division room on the north of the LUCE River should the latter find it necessary to move by that route.

14. The time of advance of Cavalry Divisions is to be decided on by the Divisional Commanders on the reports from their patrols. They are to move forward, provided the opportunity exists, once the Infantry have advanced from the GREEN Line.

15. Once the forward movement has started, the advance to the objective is to be carried out without check or pause.

16. On arrival at the objective, the line of division between the reconnaissance areas is to run from the grid line through E.16.d., through VRELY, FOUQUESCOURT, HATTENCOURT to NESLE, all inclusive to the 3rd Cavalry Division.

17. The limit to which the tanks working with Cavalry Corps are to proceed is to be the WARVILLERS, VRELY, ROSIERES-EN-SANTERRE, VAUVILLERS Road.

18. Artillery. The Infantry are to advance under a barrage up to the GREEN Line. The advance from the GREEN Line is not to be under a barrage. This means that the fighting is to take the form of semi-open warfare, and the closest co-operation between the Artillery and Infantry and Cavalry is necessary.

Heavy Artillery fire on all villages east of the RED Line and south of the railway, except LE QUESNEL, is to cease at ZERO plus 6½ hours. The fire on LE QUESNEL is to cease at Zero plus 7½ hours.

19. R.A.F.

(a) The following will be the special markings of machines on special duty :-

(i). Machines working with tanks. Black band on middle of right side of tail.

(ii). Machines working with Cavalry. Two streamers on both inside struts.

(iii). All contact patrol machines. Rectangular panels 2 ft. by 1 ft. on both lower planes about 3 foot from the fusilage.

(b).......

(b). After passing the RED Line, No.65 Squadron is to assist the Cavalry Advance by attacking ground targets.

(c). The ~~V call~~ code on Popham panel for ammunition will be used if necessary, and ammunition will be dropped by aeroplanes. Further instructions will be issued.

20. Secrecy.

(a). The necessity of secrecy is paramount. All movement of troops and transport in an easterly direction is to take place by night.

(b). Marches are to be so arranged that by daylight (4 a.m. summer time) all troops and transport are under cover.

(c). During the daytime men will remain under cover and Officers will be detailed in squadrons and other units of that size, to see that there is no movement.

(d). No reconnaissances of the ground over which the attack will take place or of bivouac areas, will take place without the sanction of Divisional Headquarters.

(e). An aeroplane is to fly over the Fourth Army area during days when flying is possible, and is to report any abnormal movement of troops or transport within our lines.

21. Communications. The Fourth Army are arranging for communication up to and inclusive of LONGEAU. From that place to CACHY, where the Headquarters of the 1st and 3rd Cavalry Divisions are to be at Zero hour, the line is to be built under A.D.Signals, Cavalry Corps. At least two lines are to be laid.

When Cavalry Corps Headquarters move from LONGEAU to CACHY, the responsibility for these communications will be taken over by the Army.

22. Advanced Cavalry Corps Headquarters is to move to YZEUX on the night of 6th/7th August. At Zero hour it is to be established at LONGEAU. On the forward move of the 1st and 3rd Cavalry Divisions, they are to move to CACHY. Further movement forward must depend on the situation.

Rear Headquarters are remaining at AUXI-LE-CHATEAU.

23. The following maps will be carried :-

1/40,000 (Enemy Sector Organization) by Officers and as many N.C.O's as possible.

1/100,000 AMIENS Sheet by all Officers and N.C.O's.

24. Gap rations will be issued in the Concentration Area.

25. Flares. RED flares are to be used by Cavalry and Infantry to mark their position, so that aeroplanes can report the points reached by our troops.

26. (a). The following will be required for duty at Corps H.Q. and will join i/a instructions to be issued later -

(i). A squadron from 3rd Cavalry Brigade.

(ii). A Liaison Officer with mounted orderlies from 4th Cavalry Brigade.

(b).......

(b). The following special Liaison Officers and patrols will be required i/a instructions to be issued later -

(i). One senior officer and 4 messengers from 5th Cavalry Brigade as liaison officer between H.Q. 3rd Cavalry Division and H.Q. 2nd Cavalry Division.

(ii). One senior officer and 4 messengers from 4th Cavalry Brigade as liaison officer between H.Q. 1st Cavalry Division and H.Q. 2nd Cavalry Division.

(iii). A patrol of 1 Officer and 6 O.R. from 5th Cavalry Brigade to work between 3rd Cavalry Division and H.Q. 2nd Cavalry Division.

(iv). A patrol of 1 Officer and 6 O.R. from 4th Cavalry Brigade to work between 1st Cavalry Division and H.Q. 2nd Cavalry Division.

(v). A patrol of 1 Officer and 6 O.R. from each Cavalry Brigade for work under Divisional Headquarters after 2nd Cavalry Division has commenced operations.

27. Roads. The AMIENS - LONGEAU - VILLERS BRETONNEUX road is to be reserved for the exclusive use of the Cavalry Corps from 9-30 p.m. on Y day to 8 a.m. on Z day. After 8 a.m. on Z day it is to be at the disposal of the Australian and Cavalry Corps. The Australian Corps is to control the traffic on it after that hour.

28. Light Signals. The following light signals are to be employed by Corps as stated :-

		Signal.	Meaning.
(i). Cavalry Corps.		White star turning to red on a parachute fired from a 1½" VERY pistol.	"Advanced troops of Cavalry are here".
(ii). III Corps.	(a)	No.32 grenade, green over green over green.	S.O.S.
	(b)	No.32 grenade, white over white over white.	Success signal, i.e. "We have reached objective".
	(c)	One white VERY light.	"Barrage is about to lift".
(iii). Canadian Corps.	(1)	No.32 grenade, red over red over red.	In addition to being employed for S.O.S. this signal will also mean - (a) "We are held up and cannot advance without help". (b) "Enemy is counter-attacking". Remark. In the case of (a) a smoke rocket (No.27 grenade) will also be fired in the direction of the obstruction to indicate its position.

(2)......

	Signal.	Meaning.
	(2). No.32 grenade, green over green over green.	(a). "Lift your fire we are going to advance". (b). "Stop firing".
	(3). Three white VERY lights in quick succession.	"We have reached this point".
(iv). Australian Corps.	(1). No.32 grenade, green over green over green.	S.O.S.
	(2). No.32 grenade, white over white over white.	Success signal, i.e. "We have reached objective".

Malise Graham

Lieut.Colonel,

General Staff.

Hd.Qrs.2nd Cavalry Divn.
6th August, 1918.

SECRET.

2nd CAVALRY DIVISION ORDER No.58.

Copy No. 4

Ref.Map 1/100,000, AMIENS.

7th August, 1918.

1. The Division will march to-night i/a March Table attached

2. Units will march in Sections, closed up without any intervals.

3.(a) Batteries will accompany Cavalry Brigades.

(b) Pack Mounted Sections C.F.A's, will accompany Brigade fighting troops.

(c) M.V.S's will accompany A.2.Echelon.

4.(a) As large numbers of other troops are moving to-night, the success of the concentration largely depends on punctuality and march discipline.

(b) There will be no lights or smoking during the march.

5. A.P.M. will assist A.P.M.Corps to clear the roads through AMIENS between 9 p.m. and 8 a.m.

6. Captain Heath's Squadron 5th Lancers will accompany 3rd Cavalry Brigade to the forward concentration area.
Captain Heath will fall out near Advanced Corps H.Q. and report to General Staff.

7. Units not mentioned in the March Table will act i/a instructions to be issued by A.A. & Q.M.G.

8. One officer of each Cavalry Brigade will after arrival in the forward concentration area reconnoitre the areas occupied by 1st and 3rd Cavalry Divisions (as per attached map) and the routes thereto.

9. The personnel for escorting prisoners of war i/a Para.4 of Table 'M' of Divisional Organization will be sent to join the A.P.M. in the forward concentration area.

10. Ref. G/161/1 - para.26.

Para. a(ii) - The Liaison Officer will report to General Staff at Advanced Corps H.Q. at 4 a.m. 8th Inst.

Para. b (i) & (ii). - The Liaison Officers and messengers will report to General Staff 3rd and 1st Cavalry Divisions respectively at their Advanced H.Q. at 1 a.m. 8th Instant.

Para. b. (iii)&(iv) - Special instructions have been communicated to officers concerned.

Para. b. (v) - The patrols will be held ready to join Divl.H.Q. as required at any time after arrival in the forward concentration area.

11.........

11. On arrival in forward concentration areas, Ammunition Column Heavy Sections will park off the road N.E. of LONGEAU.
They are not to be moved from these positions without reference to Cavalry Corps.

12. Heavy Sections of C.F.A's and A.H.T.Coy. will march to starting point in rear of Ammunition Column and will park near at hand.
They will be ready to move on receipt of orders and will be under the command of Captain J.M.GREENALL, A.S.C. who will send a Motor Cyclist D.R. to Corps H.Q. at LONGEAU at 6 a.m. on 8th Instant for orders.

13. During the March the Divisional Report Centre will be at the head of the Column.
On arrival in the forward concentration area it will be at N.E. corner of LONGEAU.
A Rear Div.H.Q. will be formed at BREILLY.

ACKNOWLEDGE.

Malise Graham

Lieut.Colonel,
General Staff, 2nd Cavalry Division.

Issued at 4 p.m.

Normal distribution.
19. Major C.R.I.NICHOLL, Oxford Hrs.
20. Major A.N.HAYWOOD, 6th Dragoon Gds.
21. Capt.J.M.GREENALL, A.H.T.Coy.
22. Ammunition Column.

March Table for night 7th/8th August. Issued with 2nd Cavalry Division Ordor No. 58.

Unit.	Starting Point.	Time.	Routo.	Bivouac.	Remarks.
Div. H.Q. H.Q.3rd Bde.R.H.A. 2nd Signal Squad.	X roads at DREUIL LES AMIENS.	12.15.a.m.	MONTIERES – railway boulevard to AMIENS main STN. – LONGEAU.	as por attachod map.	
5th Cavalry Bde.		12.20.a.m.			To S.P. via PICQUIGNY.
3rd Cavalry Bde.		12.40.a.m.			
4th Cavalry Bde.		1.0.a.m.			
2nd Field Squad.		1.20.a.m.			
Divnl.A1 Echelon.		1.25.a.m.			
Divnl.A2 Echelon.		1.35.a.m.			Follow A1 Echelon to MONTIERES X roads, thon halt and move off on tail of 1st Cav. Div.A2 Echelon.
Amm.Colm.(Heavy section)		4.45.a.m.			Follow in roar of 1st Cav.Div. Amm.Colmn.

NOTE :- 'A' Echelons will be divisionalised on the march into (A1 under Major C.R.I.NICHOLL, Q.O.O.H.)
(A2 " " A.N. HAYWOOD, 6th D.Gs.)
as under :-

Divnl.Troops	A1 Echelon follow	Field Squadron.
5th Cav.Bde.	" " "	Div.Troops A1 Echelon.
3rd Cav.Bde.	" " "	4th Cav.Bde. from PICQUIGNY to BREILLY and Fiold Squadron to AILLY.
4th Cav.Bde.	" " "	3rd Cav.Bde. A1 Echelon.
Divnl.Troops	A2 Echelon "	4th Cav.Bde. A1 Echelon.
5th Cav.Bde.	" " "	Div.Troops A2 Echelon from AILLY.
3rd Cav.Bde.	" " "	4th Cav.Bde. A1 till joining A2 Echelon of Div.Troops at BREILLY.
4th Cav.Bde.	" " "	3rd Cav.Bde. A2 Echelon.

VERY SECRET.

CORPS BOUNDARIES - BLACK DASH

GREEN LINE - 1st Objective 1st DAY.

RED LINE - 2nd OBJECTIVE 1st DAY.

BLUE LINE - 3rd OBJECTIVE 1st DAY.

RED DOTTED - FRENCH OBJECTIVE 1st DAY.

BLUE DOTTED to be secured by CAVALRY on 1st DAY.

West of this map Cavalry track is
T 6 cent. 5 Cent. 4 Cent. Road junction
3.6.3.4.

September 1918

WO 95/1127

(6339) Wt. W160/M3016 1,500,000 10/17 McA & W Ltd (E 1898) Forms W3091. Army Form W.3091.

Cover for Documents.

Nature of Enclosures.

Confidential

War Diary

of

Headquarters, 3rd Bde, R. H. A.

Volume 49

Notes, or Letters written.

HEADQUARTERS, 3RD BRIGADE, R.H.A.
No. W.D.
Date 6/10/18.

Instructions regarding War Diaries and Intelligence Summaries are contained in F. S. Regs., Part II. and the Staff Manual respectively. Title pages will be prepared in manuscript.

WAR DIARY
~~or~~
~~INTELLIGENCE~~ SUMMARY.
(*Erase heading not required.*)

Army Form C. 2118.

September 1918
3rd Brigade RHA

Place	Date	Hour	Summary of Events and Information	Remarks and references to Appendices
GAUDIEMPRÉ	1st		The whole Brigade was in billets at GAUDIEMPRÉ	LENS
	6th		Batteries marched with three Cavalry Brigades – 3rd Cavalry Brigade	1:100,000
			attached to First Army D/RHA moving to AVESNE-le-COMTE	AMIENS
			4th Cavalry Brigade remaining with 3rd Army J/RHA moving	1:100,000
			to HUMBERCOURT 5th Cavalry Brigade to 4th Army E/RHA	
			moving in to bivouacs on the ALBERT – BAPAUME road	
			Columns & Head Quarters ~~[illegible]~~ remained at GAUDIEMPRÉ	
FAMECHON	8th		Columns & Head Quarters moved to FAMECHON	
	9th		D/RHA moved to OURTON E/RHA moved to QUERRIEU	
	16th		Battery Commanders & adjutant proceeded to AUXI-le CHATEAU	
			to umpire in Cavalry Corps manoeuvres	
GAUDIEMPRÉ	17th		Cavalry Corps manoeuvres round AUXI-le CHATEAU	
			Head Quarters & Columns moved back to GAUDIEMPRE	
			Capt. Wright MC DCM RHA E/RHA posted to the	
			Riding establishment at WOOLWICH	

D. D. & L., London, E.C.
(A7883) Wt. W809/M1672 350,000 4/17 Sch. 52a. Forms/C/2118/14

Instructions regarding War Diaries and Intelligence Summaries are contained in F. S. Regs., Part II. and the Staff Manual respectively. Title pages will be prepared in manuscript.

WAR DIARY
or
INTELLIGENCE SUMMARY.
(Erase heading not required.)

HQrs 3rd Brigade R.H.A. Army Form C. 2118.
September 1918

Place	Date	Hour	Summary of Events and Information	Remarks and references to Appendices
GAUDIEMPRE	17th -21st		Routine & training	
			Capt. Wright H.C. DCM R.H.A. left E Battery to join the Reserve Establishment at Woolwich	
			Lieut G.F. Elliot MC appointed Captain of E Battery R.H.A.	
			Lt Col A. Mellor D.S.O. R.H.A. returned from leave to U.K.	
	27th		News received that E Battery R.H.A. had left OVERRIEU for PROYART with 5th Cavalry Brigade	
	28th		G.O.C. R.H.A. visited Brigade Head Quarters	
	29th		Routine	
	30th		Evening of 30th. Captain Bond 2Lt Roddick and 26 men from Column left by motor lorry to join E. Battery who were short of men.	

D. Mellor Lt Col RHA
Cmd 3rd Bde RHA

D. D. & L., London, E.C.
(A10266) Wt W5300/P713 750,000 2/18 Sch. 52 Forms/C2118/16.

W0 95/28

(6339) Wt. W160/M3016 1,500,000 10/17 McA & W Ltd (E 1898) Forms W3091. Army Form W.3091.

Cover for Documents.

Nature of Enclosures.

Confidential

War-Diary

of

Headquarters, 3rd Brigade, R.H.A.

~ for ~

October 1918

Volume ~~49~~ 50

Notes, or Letters written.

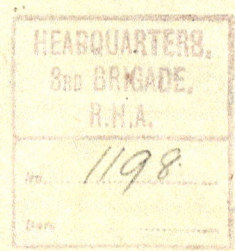

HEADQUARTERS,
3RD BRIGADE,
R.H.A.
No. 1198
Date

October 1918

WAR DIARY
~~or~~
~~INTELLIGENCE SUMMARY.~~
(Erase heading not required.)

Head Quarters
3rd Brigade R.H.A.
2nd Cavalry Division

Army Form C. 2118.

Instructions regarding War Diaries and Intelligence Summaries are contained in F. S. Regs., Part II, and the Staff Manual respectively. Title pages will be prepared in manuscript.

Place	Date	Hour	Summary of Events and Information	Remarks and references to Appendices
GAUDIEMPRÉ	October 1918, 1st		Head Quarters, Column in billets at GAUDIEMPRE	Ref sheet LENS 11. 1/100000
			Batteries detached with their Cavalry Brigades. D/RHA at INCHY. J/RHA at MASNIERES. E/RHA with 5th Cavalry Brigade, in action under 9th Corps, in vicinity of BELLENGLISE	ST QUENTIN 1:100,000
			Work at Head Quarters, Column consisted of routine and improvements carried out on Horse Standings.	
	8th		HQrs telephone cart was sent to be attached to 5th Cavalry Brigade Signal Troop, joined the Brigade near BOHAIN.	
	14th		Capt. J.A.M. Bond R.H.A. returned from E Battery R.H.A. which had come out of action the previous day, but remained near BOHAIN under 9th Corps.	
			Major S.R. Wason M.C. R.H.A. was wounded on 2nd inst. and evacuated & Major G.G. Simpson M.C. R.H.A. took over the command of E Battery on 14th inst.	
			Major R.C.F. Maitland D.S.O. R.H.A. left J Battery on promotion & was succeeded by Major K. Willett M.C. R.H.A.	

D. D. & L., London, E.C.
(A7883) Wt. W803/M1672 350,000 3/17 Sch. 52a Forms/C/2118/14

Instructions regarding War Diaries and Intelligence Summaries are contained in F. S. Regs., Part II. and the Staff Manual respectively. Title pages will be prepared in manuscript.

WAR DIARY ~~or INTELLIGENCE SUMMARY.~~

(Erase heading not required.)

October 1918

Head Quarters 3rd Brigade RHA

Army Form C. 2118.

Place	Date	Hour	Summary of Events and Information	Remarks and references to Appendices
GAUDIEMPRÉ	Oct. 14th - 31st		T Battery moves to CREVECOEUR. D Battery remained at INCHY	LENS
			E Battery after being in action again on 18th inst in support	VALENCIENNES
			of 9th Corps Infantry attack, moved to BECQUIGNY.	1:100,000
			Column: Head Quarters in billets at GAUDIEMPRÉ	
			on 22nd inst Lieut C T E Robinson RHA left D Battery on	
			promotion to Captain, to join T Battery RHA	

Tamp[illegible] Capt RHA
for Lt Col. comdg 3rd Brigade RHA

VR 29

Confidential.

War Diary

of

H.Q., 3rd Brigade R.H.A.

November, 1918 - Volume LI.

Instructions regarding War Diaries and Intelligence Summaries are contained in F. S. Regs., Part II. and the Staff Manual respectively. Title pages will be prepared in manuscript.

WAR DIARY ~~or~~ ~~INTELLIGENCE SUMMARY.~~

(Erase heading not required.)

Army Form C. 2118.

Head Quarters 3rd Brigade R H A
November 1918

Place	Date	Hour	Summary of Events and Information	Remarks and references to Appendices
	November 1918.			
GAUDIEMPRE	1st		Lt Col A Mellor DSO RHA proceeded on Artillery Course in U.K.	Lens 1:100,000
	1st-5th		In billets at GAUDIEMPRE. Batteries detached with their Cavalry Brigades	"
	6th		Marched to BIHUCOURT near BAPAUME wet day long march	"
	7th		Marched to CAMBRAI & billeted in Cavalry Barracks there	"
	11th		Heard news that armistice had been signed. D/RHA was in action near MONS this morning. Orders received for 2nd Cavalry Div to concentrate near MAUBEUGE & to be prepared to act as advance Guard to IVth Army in the advance of the Army of occupation to the Rhine	VALENCIENNES 1:100,000
	13th		Marched to BOUSIES & billeted there for night	
	14th		Marched to TAISNIERES	

D. D. & L., London, E.C.
(A10266) Wt.W5300/P713 750,000 2/18 Sch. 52 Forms/C2118/16.

Instructions regarding War Diaries and Intelligence Summaries are contained in F. S. Regs., Part II. and the Staff Manual respectively. Title pages will be prepared in manuscript.

WAR DIARY
~~INTELLIGENCE SUMMARY.~~
(*Erase heading not required.*)

Army Form C. 2118.

Head Quarters
3rd Brigade RHA
November 1918

Place	Date	Hour	Summary of Events and Information	Remarks and references to Appendices
	November 1918			
TAISMIERES	15th		Marched to DOUZIES on W. outskirts of MAUBEUGE. Lt Col Mellor who had been recalled rejoined the Brigade here & the division concentrated in the vicinity	VALENCIENNES 1:100 000
DOUZIES	17th		Marched to THUIN. Very enthusiastic reception from inhabitants everywhere along the road & in billets	NAMUR 1:100 000
THUIN	18th		Marched to MORIALME	
MORIALME	21st		marched to DINANT.	
DINANT	~~19th~~ 22nd		Marched to BARCINALLE	
BARCINALLE	23rd		Marched to WAHA near MARCHE	MARCHE 1:100 000
WAHA	24th		Adjutant inspected a large number of captured German Guns etc	
	24th - 31st		In billets at Marche. E/RHA proceeding with 5th Cavalry Brigade as advance Guard to Canadian Corps into Germany	

Tom ? Capt RHA
for Lt Col Comdg 3rd Brigade RHA

D. D. & L., London, E.C.
(A10266) Wt W5300/P713 750,000 2/18 Sch. 52 Forms/C2118/16.

(6392) Wt. W6192/P875 1,500,000 4/18 McA & W Ltd (E 2815) Forms W3091/4. Army Form W.3091.

WO 95/1130

Cover for Documents.

Nature of Enclosures.

CONFIDENTIAL

W A R D I A R Y

of

Headquarters, 3rd Brigade R.H.A.

From 1st December, 1918

To 31st December, 1918.

VOLUME L11.

=*=*=*=*=*=*=*=*=*=*=*=*=*

Notes, or Letters written.

December 1918.

Instructions regarding War Diaries and Intelligence Summaries are contained in F. S. Regs., Part II, and the Staff Manual respectively. Title pages will be prepared in manuscript.

HEADQUARTERS, 3RD BRIGADE, R.H.A.
No.
Date.

WAR DIARY or INTELLIGENCE SUMMARY.

(Erase heading not required.)

Army Form C. 2118.

Head Quarters 3rd Brigade R.H.A. 2nd Cavalry Division

Place	Date	Hour	Summary of Events and Information	Remarks and references to Appendices
WAHA	December 1st–16th		In billets at WAHA.	MARCHE
			Nothing of importance to record.	1:100,000.
	16th		Marched from MARCHE to BOMAL.	
	17th		Marched to HODBOMONT near THEUX.	LIEGE 1:100000
	28th		Lt Col A. Mellor D.S.O. R.H.A. Major E.F. Norton D.S.O. M.C. R.H.A. cmdg D/R.H.A. Captain T.A.M. Bond R.H.A. adjutant 3rd Brigade R.H.A. Lieut T.N.H. Wilson R.H.A. D/R.H.A. Sergt. CHARLETT 3rd Brigade R.H.A. Ammunition Column and Corporal T.F. Townsend Head Quarters 3rd Brigade R.H.A. were "mentioned in despatches" (Sir D. Haig's Despatch of Nov 8th 1918)	
			The time in billets is being spent in education & demobilisation schemes, & in general routine.	
			Men & horses all comfortably billeted and the horses throughout the Brigade in excellent condition.	
			The end of Dec. finds the Brigade still up to fighting strength and a thoroughly efficient unit in every way	
			T.A.M. Bond Captain R.H.A.	

(A7883) D. D. & L., London, E.C. Wt. W803/M1672 350,000 4/17 Sch. 52a Forms/C/2118/14

(6392) Wt. W6192/P875 1,500,000 4/18 McA & W Ltd E 2815 Form ...

W 95 / 1131

Cover for Documents.

CONFIDENTIAL.

Nature of Enclosures.

WAR DIARY

of

Headquarters, 3rd Brigade R.H.A.

2nd Cavalry Division

From 1st to 31st January, 1919.

VOLUME 53.

Notes, or Letters written.

Instructions regarding War Diaries and Intelligence Summaries are contained in F. S. Regs., Part II. and the Staff Manual respectively. Title pages will be prepared in manuscript.

Jan. 1919

WAR DIARY ~~or~~ ~~INTELLIGENCE SUMMARY~~.

(*Erase heading not required.*)

Head Quarters 3rd Brigade R.H.A.

Army Form C. 2118.

Place	Date	Hour	Summary of Events and Information	Remarks and references to Appendices
HODBOMONT	January 1919		The unit spent the whole of January in billets at HODBOMONT	LIEGE 1:100000
			Personnel of all units in the Brigade is being steadily	
			demobilised & as the men are going while the horses remain	
			all units are shorthanded and nothing more than	
			the ordinary routine of exercise stables water & feed can	
			be attempted	
			The horses all look well & the men remained contented	
			& well disciplined.	
			E Battery R.H.A. won the Seligman ~~Cup~~ Football cup open to	
			all the R.H.A. of the Cavalry Corps during the month	
			and 5143 Francs were collected from the Brigade as	
			subscriptions to the Royal Artillery War Commemoration Fund	
			[signature] Capt. R.H.A.	
			Adjutant 3rd Brigade R.H.A.	

D. D. & L., London, E.C. (A7883) Wt. W809/M1672 350,000 4/17 Sch. 52a Forms/C/2118/14

C O N F I D E N T I A L.

WAR DIARY

of

Headquarters, 3rd Brigade R.H.A.

From 1st to 28th February, 1919.

VOLUME 54.

Instructions regarding War Diaries and Intelligence Summaries are contained in F. S. Regs., Part II. and the Staff Manual respectively. Title pages will be prepared in manuscript.

WAR DIARY
or
INTELLIGENCE SUMMARY.
(Erase heading not required.)

HEADQUARTERS.
3rd BRIGADE R.H.A.

Army Form C. 2118.

Place	Date	Hour	Summary of Events and Information	Remarks and references to Appendices
Hodbomont. Theux. Belgium.	1919. Feby.		The Unit spent the whole of February in billets at HODBOMONT-Theux. Personnel of all Units of the Brigade is being steadily demobilized. Horses of the Brigade being also demobilized and sold to Belgians. "D" Battery R.H.A. "J" Battery R.H.A. and Ammunition Column of 3rd Brigade R.H.A. together with Headquarters, are being reduced to Cadre Strength, preparatory to embarking for England. "E" Battery R.H.A. have been ordered to form one of the Batteries R.H.A. for the 1st Cavalry Division, for Army of Occupation. Nothing more than ordinary routine of exercise, stables etc can be reported. The men remain well disciplined and controlled. HEADQUARTERS, 3RD BRIGADE, R.H.A. D Muller Lt. Col. R.H.A. O.C., 3rd Brigade R.H.A.	

D. D. & L., London, E.C.
(A10266) Wt W5300/P713 750,000 2/18 Sch. 52 Forms/C2118/16.

www.ingramcontent.com/pod-product-compliance
Lightning Source LLC
Chambersburg PA
CBHW080855230426
43662CB00013B/2109